THIS BOOK IS GAY

JUNO DAWSON

Illustrations by Spike Gerrell · Introduction by David Levithan

sourcebooks
fire

Published by Sourcebooks Fire, an imprint of Sourcebooks
P.O. Box 4410, Naperville, Illinois 60567-4410
(630) 961-3900
sourcebooks.com

Originally published in 2015 by Sourcebooks Fire, an imprint of Sourcebooks.

Library of Congress Cataloging-in-Publication data is on file with the publisher.

Printed and bound in the United States of America.
VP 11 10 9 8

This book is dedicated to anyone who has ever wondered.

Contents

THIS INTRODUCTION IS GAY

(BUT IT TOOK SOME TIME TO GET HERE)
by David Levithan

So, yeah, I was pretty oblivious.

Even though I had kissed boys (and liked it). Even though other people had called me gay (rarely as a compliment). Even though my friends had asked if I was gay (later, I found out it was okay that I was). Even though it was pictures of guys that turned me on (I had a stash). Even though I had a gay uncle who brought his boyfriend to Thanksgiving (without incident). Even though all the signs were there—I still didn't make the connection. I was—what's the phrase? Willfully ignorant.

What I'm saying is: Even though it was obvious, it took me a while to figure out I was gay.

Granted, now is a different time. At this point, even five years ago is a different time.

But the timeless reason I was so clueless was this: I couldn't recognize the clues.

And since I didn't recognize them, I couldn't find them. Until I did.

For me, it was a quote in my college newspaper. A fellow student was interviewed about how he knew he was gay. And his answer was simple—he said that whenever he fantasized, he thought about being with guys.

And I thought: *Oh, yeah. That. Hmm.*

I gathered more clues. I pieced together more answers. It got easier and easier.

I was fine.

No, better than that.

I was who I was meant to be.

When I was in high school, there's no way a book like this would have made it to me. But what if it had? I imagine I would have figured out things sooner. I would have been less clueless—because this is, if nothing else, an extraordinarily helpful book of clues. And here's the thing about clues: They don't tell you what to do, but they do show you what you *can* do.

This book is gay...but you don't have to be gay in order to read it. Whether you're curious about the gay people in your life (clue: They're there!), questioning your own identity, or very sure of your own identity (thank you very much) but a little lost in the ins and outs of...well, the ins and outs—this is a crash course to prevent you from crashing, the honest truths in a world where there are few simple truths.

I've been gay longer than any current teenager has been alive (pauses, freaks out a little), but I still found a new clue or two. Or two dozen.

When I travel, I love to read guidebooks first to hear what other people have to say about where I'm going before I get there. Then when I arrive, I close the guidebooks and have my own experience of the place. So, think of this as a handy guidebook. Take in what it has to say. See what it helps you figure out. Then close it, and experience.

I promise: There's a lot to experience.

Author's Note

Welcome to the updated edition of *This Book is Gay*! This book, first released in 2014, has taken the world by storm. It's been translated into a dozen languages; it's been banned in Alaska; it's hit the headlines in the UK.

More importantly, I've received hundreds upon hundreds of letters, tweets, and emails from all over the world—from young people *and* their parents, either asking for guidance or thanking me for writing the book. That was the dream when the book first came out, so it has been a dream come true.

But the world doesn't stand still for very long and it became clear that some of the facts in the previous edition were rapidly becoming out of touch. This revised edition takes into account shifting awareness of issues surrounding both sexuality and gender. I've also listened to feedback—that some readers felt excluded or sidelined, which was never the intent.

My life has changed too. *I've* now lived as both James

and Juno, and have new perspectives on life as a transgender woman.

As with the first edition, some contributor names have been changed or left out, and I've used LGBTQ+ as a quick shorthand that I intend to include all queer/nonbinary people inclusively.

In challenging times, it's more important than ever that we come together as a community and support one another. It all starts with kindness, compassion and *you*.

Juno x

The *This Book Is Gay* survey was carried out in spring/summer 2013. From the three hundred respondents, case studies were chosen and interviewed more thoroughly. Some names have been changed to protect the confidentiality of some interviewees. A huge thank-you to all who took part.

CHAPTER 1

WELCOME TO THE MEMBERS' CLUB

LESSON ONE

- Sometimes men like men.
- Sometimes women like women.
- Sometimes women like men and women.
- Sometimes men like women and men.
- Sometimes people don't like anyone.
- Sometimes a man might want to be a woman.
- Sometimes a woman might want to be a man.
- Sometimes people don't identify as a man or as a woman.

Got that? It really is that simple.

I could end the lesson there, but I don't think a few pages would make a very good book, so I *suppose* I should go into a bit more depth...

WELCOME TO THE MEMBERS' CLUB

There's a long-running joke that, on "coming out," a young lesbian, gay guy, bisexual, or trans person should receive a membership card and instruction manual.

THIS IS THAT INSTRUCTION MANUAL.

You're welcome. But this is a manual for everyone—no matter your gender or sexual preference.

School probably hasn't taught you very much about what it's like to be lesbian, gay, bisexual, trans, or questioning. You might have heard about famous gay people or seen same-sex couples on TV. You almost certainly know an LGBTQ+ person, even if you aren't aware of it. Like an "alien invasion," we are already among you. We serve you in the post office; we teach you math; we make your hamburgers.

So why don't we teach you about same-sex couples when we teach sex ed? Or that a lot of people choose their gender? Well, I was a PSHCE (Personal, Social, Health, and Citizenship Education) teacher in the UK for a long time, and I always taught my students about these things, but not all schools do, and not all teachers know how—there's NO training for this, I'm afraid.

I surveyed a group of more than three hundred young

people in 2012, and 95 percent of them said their school taught them NOTHING about gay sex as a part of sex education. Sex between men and women was routinely presented as "the norm."

This lack of education means that loads of young people—gay, straight, or bi; trans or cis—have oodles of questions about what it's like to be LGBTQ+. This book has some of the answers. Whether you think you might be LGBTQ+ or you think you're straight but have questions or you're anywhere in between, this book is for you.

Your sexuality and gender are very much individual things, but what if there were a whole bunch of people who'd been through it all before to mentor you through this funny old patch?

The awareness that your sexual or gender identity isn't quite the NORM can be a confusing, exciting, exhilarating, concerning, and, frankly, baffling time. Long before you "come out" and tell people about your identity, it's just you and your brain trying to figure it out, so it can also be a lonely time, often accompanied by whiny music and too much eyeliner.

My past experience as a gay, white man and, more recently, as a trans white woman is not representative of every gay man or trans woman, let alone the thousands of gay women, bisexual men and women, and trans people who may be reading this book.

Therefore, before writing this book, I searched far and wide for dozens of other LGBTQ+ people to share their experiences with you. Individually, we can never know it all, but together we're quite wise, like that baboon in *The Lion King*.

I haven't edited or changed the testimonies of the LGBTQ+ people in this book, so you might not identify or agree with everything they have to say, AND THAT'S FINE. We have to be able to talk about sexuality and identity in a nonhysterical way.

Sexuality and gender are individual experiences; people are entitled to opinions and, vitally, we need to be able to make mistakes. I understand identity is an issue that some people feel very strongly about. This is also a good thing—activism is what got us this far—but if people aren't allowed to say what's really on their minds for fear of upsetting people, we'll end up never saying anything at all.

In short, we have to be able to laugh at ourselves, whatever our identity, or we're in for a long-haul life. So, yeah, *This Book Is Gay* isn't entirely serious all the way through (although we do deal with some MEGA SAD FACE topics).

This is something different to the loads of dreary textbooks about gender and sexuality politics that are already out there. This book is serious, but it's also fun and funny.

The whole point of coming out is that we have the FREEDOM to be who we are. When did that stop being FUN?

If you're new to the club, you're lucky because being L or G or B or T or Q or + is SUPER FUN. You're FREE now and don't have to HIDE.

Whatever you identify as by the end of this book, you'll see that, far from being alone, you're joining a vast collective of cool, happy, inspirational people, each with a story to tell.

It's the hippest members club in town, and you get straight past the velvet rope and into the VIP lounge.

You're not isolated; you're part of something bigger now. Something great.

OH, HI, SEXTHOUGHTS

Let's start at the very beginning (a very good place to start). I guess you're reading this book for one of several reasons. It may be because you already identify as LGBTQ+ (and, let's face it, we love nothing more than talking about it). Maybe you're nosy to see what we get up to between the sheets. It could be you are making fun of it because it has the word "gay" in the title (shame on you). But maybe, just maybe, you picked up this book because you're WONDERING.

It all starts with wondering.

Wondering what it might be like to kiss that boy or what that girl's breasts look like. What life would be like if you were a girl, not a guy. It's all about wondering.

Wondering is perfectly natural but never encouraged.

One day I was in the park sunbathing. On the next picnic blanket over, a mother was talking to her son about the things he could do when he was older. The conversation went something like this:

Boy: Drive a car!

Mom: Yes!

Boy: Go to work like Daddy!

Mom: Yes!

Boy: Kissing!

Mom: Yes! Girls...you'll kiss girls.

After I had snatched the child away and left him with social services (OK, I didn't do that, but I probably should have done something other than tut really loudly), I was sad at how we still DEFAULT to heterosexual in the twenty-first century.

The assumption goes that all babies are born both straight and locked into their birth gender unless something goes awry.

This is NOT the case.

- In a 2018 Gallup Poll, the percentage of American adults identifying as LGBTQ+ was 4.5 percent, which equates to more than 11 million people—roughly the number of people who live in Ohio!
- A 2016 Williams Institute study estimates there are just over 1.3 million transgender adults living in the U.S.

And yet we're all automatically born "straight" and "cis" (the gender we're assigned at birth).

Let's do sexuality first. You are told you're straight and assume you're straight for almost all of your childhood, despite quite compelling feelings to the contrary. You believe yourself to be straight (because isn't everyone?) until sexual desire kicks in (assuming it does). I like to call this desire SEXTHOUGHTS.

Because most of us spend our childhood identifying as straight, even though we may or may not actually feel straight, we don't always identify these sexthoughts. But it seems highly likely that from a very young age we, as LGBTQ+ people, were attracted to members of the same sex, be it people we know or shiny TV people. (Well, they are pretty hot, right?)

I wanted to know at what stage LGBTQ+ people first had questioning thoughts regarding their sexuality OR gender. So I surveyed hundreds of them.

See figure 1. (Who said statistics had to be boring? Look how pretty that pie chart is!)

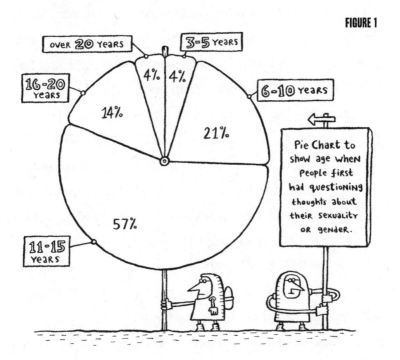

FIGURE 1

As you can see, almost a quarter of the sample were having same-sex sexthoughts and/or thoughts regarding their gender before puberty, with over half at puberty.

This makes sense, because puberty is the time at which great changes occur. One big change is the hormonal shift that drives us toward sexual relationships. It is at this point that many of us realize the cheeky little thoughts we're having late at night might be about people with the same bits as us. ESCÁNDALO.

For me it was Dean Cain. Dean Cain, as if you don't know, is the very handsome actor who played Clark Kent in *Lois and Clark: The New Adventures of Superman*. Up until Cain came into my life, I had been convinced I was going to marry Kelly, a girl in my class (whose name I have changed for her protection), because she was kind, friendly, and blond.

However, what I felt for Dean Cain (whose name I did *not* change for this book—I mean, I think IT'S TIME HE KNEW OF MY LOVE) was VERY different to what I felt for Kelly.

My interest in spandex-clad arms was far more pressing than being *fond* of Kelly, and when Clark got together with Lois, I felt the most intense jealousy of my life. (I TOTALLY get how the BTS ARMY feels on Twitter.)

Later, after a massive crush on a male teacher, I had to acknowledge that these feelings went beyond mere appreciation of the male form and were, in fact, sexthoughts. At the time, I was supposed to be a boy, and this had huge implications for my identity.

Oh, Shit!

When first faced with same-sex sexthoughts, or sexthoughts about your gender, your first reaction may well be the above. After all, society, films, television, newspapers, and books have told you your whole life that

$$STRAIGHT = NORMAL$$
$$NOT\ STRAIGHT = NOT\ NORMAL$$

You have suddenly identified a sexthought that is different. And most people don't like different so, therefore, you're slapped with the NOT NORMAL label.

Don't panic.

Just because LGBTQ+ people are in a minority, it doesn't mean they are not NORMAL. People with blue eyes are in the minority too, but we don't think of them as abnormal, do we? We don't look at Jake Gyllenhaal and say, LOOK AT THAT MASSIVE, BLUE-EYED FREAK! No, we only look at him and weep that we cannot have him. Anyway, who gets to decide what's "normal" and what isn't? What a horrid, excluding word that is.

You may have grown up not only in the absence of gay or trans role models, but also encountering actual homophobia or transphobia. These things can be hugely worrying—especially at a time when you rely on familial support. You may also be one of the thousands of people born with same-sex sexthoughts in a country where it is illegal to have sexual activity with same-sex partners. (Some people believe same-sex activity is against their religion. More on that in chapter 6.)

You probably have questions. I had LOADS of questions. I'd heard RUMORS about what two men did together. You may have misunderstood things—my early concept of lesbian sex was way off. (I basically thought it was like sanding the boobs off two Barbie dolls by rubbing them together.) You may have seen odd bits on TV and now don't know what to think. It seems highly likely that any sex ed you had at school taught you only how men and women make babies together and didn't mention transgender people at all.

WHY ARE THERE TRANS PEOPLE IN THIS BOOK?

You are right to ask this. Lesbian, gay, bisexual, and the other orientations we talk about in this book are about sexuality.

Being transgender has nothing to do with who you want to do sexytime with—it's about gender.

Trans people and nonstraight people are subject to a lot of the same discrimination, misunderstanding, and mistreatment, because many people think of us as all being part of the same group. In a way, we are—and that's why many people use "LGBTQ+" as shorthand for our whole community. That initialism is inclusive of "trans," so this manual should be too.

When people go through gender transition, their sexual feelings may or may not change too. This means that some transgender people are also gay or lesbian. Those people may have to contend with both transphobia AND homophobia, so they need twice the support.

What's more, if we wanted to, we all could spend our lives hiding. Initially, when I was living as James, I could have lied and pretended to fancy girls. Later, once I better understood my true gender, I could have lied and pretended to be a man. But I didn't. Twice, I did something about it and came out of hiding. So do *all* out proud visible LGBTQ+ people. Not always the easy choice, but the *right* one.

So whether it's L, G, B, T, or Q, or a combination of them, we're all seeking membership to this awesome club that exists outside the majority. And that's why we're all in this (book) together.

THiNGS No oNE sayS EVER

When did you realize you were straight?

Does your mom know you're straight?

When you have straight sex, is one of you the woman?

I have a straight friend—would you like me to set you up on a date?

It was so much fun—we went dancing at a straight club!

I went to the cutest straight wedding this weekend.

Do you think straight people should be allowed to have kids?

I don't mind straight people kissing, but I wish they wouldn't rub our faces in it.*

---

* There is a special place in Hades for ALL people—gay, straight, or otherwise— who kiss with visible tongue/audible slurping in public places.

CHAPTER 2
THE NAME GAME

So, you may have SEXTHOUGHTS about people of the same gender as you, OR you may have questions regarding your own gender. Loads of people—even people who end up identifying as straight and cis—have these thoughts and questions. I think it's far odder to have NEVER thought about it. I only fancy blokes, but I've considered having sexyfuntime with women plenty of times. It looks like fab fun, but just...not for me. I wish I *were* more pansexual.

This is all fine. The fact that you've identified your sexthoughts is probably the hardest part, so reward yourself with a delicious piece of cake.

BUT now we get to the bit where you actually have to make a choice.

1. You can choose to do nothing. You can sit on these feelings and hope they go away.
2. You can acknowledge them and act on them—have the sex you wanna have or wear the clothes you wanna wear—but choose not to define yourself.
3. You can act on them AND adopt an identity to define yourself. This is the bit where you'd get the membership card and become part of a community.

Wowsers, this whole gay thing is a lot more complicated than *Glee* led us to believe.

People with same-sex sexthoughts or uncertainty about their gender sometimes stop at option one, but I think these people are probably very sad and angry. (I also think a lot of crazy homophobes are lingering perilously close to option one, and this is what makes them so hateful. Freud called it "transference." This basically means that you hate in others what you hate about yourself.)

More people choose option two—you can **totally** have sex with people who are the same gender as you and not be "gay" or "lesbian" or "bi." This is why a lot of forms (especially medical ones) you fill in may refer to "men who have sex with men," etc.

You have very little choice about your sexual preferences or gender, but only you get to define yourself. This is option three: You get to be out and proud and open about your relationships or gender. Living with stress and secrets is stressful.

It's human nature to label things, and if you're having some confusing thoughts, giving a name to the situation may make you feel better because you can be part of something—a bigger support network—the International Haus of Gay, if you will.

I present the identity machine. Start at the top and see where it takes you!

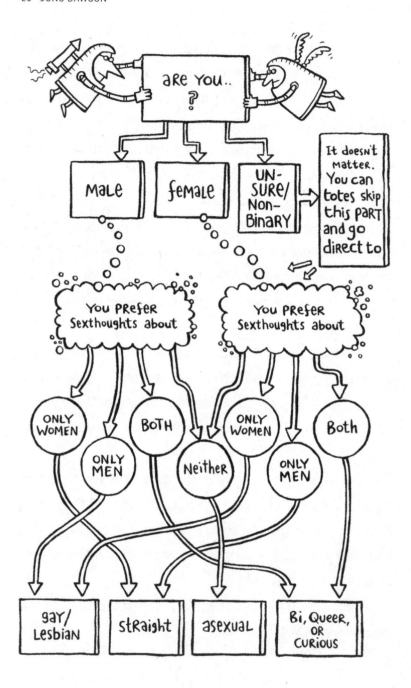

SEX PIGEONS

Before we go any further, you'll note I use the word "prefer." Sexuality and gender identity are very much about preference. I think we all CONSIDER sex with both men and women.

Like I said, why wouldn't we? We're surrounded by sexy images in magazines and on TV. People who say they haven't thought about it are probably liars. Therefore, it's all about what we prefer sexually. We need to be open-minded at all times.

It's also worth noting that there are stacks of folks who don't like any of the above sexuality options. There are loads of pigeonholes to stuff people into, but not everyone fits into them so easily.

Your identity is as individual as your fingerprints. Frankly, if you want to identify as a carrot, I will march in the Carrot Pride parade with you. Your identity is your business. It's all gravy.

Now that we've been label shopping, it's worth noting that the one you bought has a return policy. Sexual preference and gender are **fluid**, meaning just because you feel one way now, it doesn't necessarily mean you'll feel the same way in five years' time. Plenty of people change their sexual identity, and that's fine. In fact, when this book was first published, I was a gay man. Now I'm a trans woman! That's just the way it goes, ain't it.

So if everything's changeable, and if we all exist on a fluctuating, wibbly-wobbly spectrum of sexual desire (something very hard to define at the best of times), why do we bother with labels at all? Why don't we all just skip around with flowers in our hair, making out with the people we like, regardless of their gender?

Well, probably because that's quite hard to describe. At the end of the day, it's easier to have a single word to use to define yourself when talking to other people. People will ask you how you identify and, although it's tempting to launch into a tirade about the tyranny of labels, it's far simpler to say, "Oh, I'm bi," and let that be it. Still, even that doesn't mean you HAVE to adopt a label; plenty of people don't.

With this in mind, let's take a look at the most common labels on offer at the Identity Shop.

L IS FOR LESBIAN

The word lesbian is derived from the name of the island of Lesbos, where a Greek poet called Sappho ran her own sixth-century BCE version of *The L Word*. She gathered a whole gang of girls in the sunshine and wrote poems about how hot they were. Fast-forward twenty-five hundred years, to around the turn of the twentieth century, and women were seeking a name for a growing subculture that was gaining visibility and status. Until this point, historically, gay women were almost considered a myth—probably a sign of how little women were regarded or thought of as sexual creatures outside of marriage.

But now, gay women, inspired by Sappho's island of lusty ladies, coined the name "lesbian," which before then had been used to describe anything "of Lesbos."

100%
Attracted To
MEN

Today the word more or less means "a woman who has sex with women." Some such women don't like the word "lesbian" and prefer "gay woman."

> I prefer "gay" to "lesbian"—I think it's something about the noun vs. adjective thing, i.e., "lesbian" sounds a bit more central and defining, whereas "gay" is just one of a number of adjectives that could be used to describe a person.
>
> —J, 28, Brighton, UK

Now. You may have heard some people calling lesbians "dykes." This is a touchy subject because it originated as an insulting term. **Unless you identify as lesbian yourself, you should never use the word "dyke" at all.** The word is pejorative unless it's being reclaimed as slang by gay women themselves.

G IS FOR GAY

The word "gay" started life meaning joyful, carefree, bright, and showy, from the French term "gaiety," which is still used.

However, by the seventeenth century, the word had evolved: A "gay woman" was a prostitute, a "gay man" was promiscuous, and a "gay house" was a brothel. Nice.

So, by the mid-twentieth century, gay still meant "carefree"—as opposed to those who were "straight" or a little square—and started to take on its homosexual connotations. Given that at the time, "homosexual" was a clinical diagnosis, it's no wonder that a term meaning "bright and showy" ironically became shorthand for men who wished to exist in a secret subculture.

By the 1990s, it was decided that "gay" was the preferred and politically correct way to refer to men who have sex with men (and, of course, also women who have sex with women).

Sadly, at about the same time, the word "gay" was also twisted to mean something that was weak, crap, or trash. I don't care what anyone says, this usage stems from homophobia, so don't do it. YES, I KNOW IT'S IN THE TITLE, BUT THAT'S BECAUSE I'M MAKING A POINT— EVERYTHING IN THIS BOOK IS ABOUT ACTUALLY BEING GAY (or lesbian or bi or trans or queer or +, but that wouldn't have been nearly as attention grabbing, would it?).

B IS FOR BISEXUAL

This is nothing new. The people of ancient Greece and Rome were generally pansexual (people who are sexually attracted to people regardless of their gender or sexuality), and no one batted an eyelid. Sadly for us, we like things to be binary: black/ white, good/bad, male/female. And this isn't great for anyone.

Broadly speaking, a bisexual is someone who like to have sex with people of two (or more) genders: men, women, and nonbinary folks too. There are a plethora of misunderstandings about bisexuality, the most prevalent being the "bi now, gay later" theory that all gay men and lesbians have a brief period in Bi-Town before catching the last train to Gayville. While this is the case for some actual gay men and women, there are plenty of people who have no intention of traveling all the way to the end of the line. AND THAT'S FINE.

The idea that bisexual people "are kidding themselves" or that they are "being selfish" and/or "greedy" is hurtful. Why is it so hard to accept that someone might be attracted to both sexes? If someone is willing to identify as bi, then surely they'd be just as happy to wear a "gay" label. What would be the point in lying? Why do we so badly need people to be gay or straight? Bisexual people might be misunderstood, but they have the right to be PROUD of their identity and sexual preference.

> I identify as lesbian, because I don't like to admit I'm bisexual.
>
> —Blaz, 34, Bristol, UK

I identify as bisexual, though I rather like to describe it as "People are beautiful, people are hot, people are attractive, and if I fall in love, I fall in love."
—Mickey, 18, Michigan

I tell people I'm bi because it's easier to understand, but I think I'm pan—I'm concerned with personality, not genitals.
—Anon, 24, Brighton, UK

[I say I'm] bisexual when asked. Varies depending on the day, who I've been around, what I've been reading, and so on. A description I found on Tumblr that fits perfectly goes along the lines of "If you think of sexuality in terms of music, where the low notes represent being attracted to boys and high notes represent being attracted to girls, I am a Slayer guitar solo."
—Nina, 16, UK

Q IS FOR QUEER

"Queer" originally meant someone or something a little unusual or out of the ordinary. In the late twentieth century, it became a derogatory term or abuse word aimed at homosexuals.

However, more recently, following the AIDS pandemic, the word was reclaimed (at first by the group Queer Nation) as a catchall phrase to represent the full spectrum of sexuality and gender but later as more of a criticism of identity than an identity itself. Basically a label for people—gay or straight—who were sick of labels!

Nonetheless, it is now used as an identity. In the broadest possible terms, as there are a number of groups under the "queer" umbrella, being queer means not having to define your sexual identity or gender with just one label.

In a world in which your sexuality and gender are open to change, it does sometimes seem silly to use labels. Even classing yourself as bisexual adds to the idea that there are only three choices, which clearly isn't the case—nor should it be an automatic term for someone who is neither gay nor straight.

Queer theory is a fascinating and expanding subject, and there are many, many books and theses written on it.

> Defining yourself with a deliberately slippery word might seem like a contradiction in terms. For me, that was the point. I feel that "straight," "gay," and "bi" don't adequately cover or include the way I feel.
>
> For one thing, those terms suggest a rigid and inflexible take on gender. For people who see sex and

gender in any way other than binaries, the options of "one, the other, or both" simply don't fit.

In addition to that, I find that gender/sex is a relatively small part of sexual attraction for me. It seems odd to define my sexual identity by a small facet of it. While some people—some LGBT people or people into kink, for example—choose to solve this problem with more specific identities, I'd rather not try and sum it up in that way.

For me, identifying as queer is a way of placing myself outside straight, mainstream sexuality without having to identify with other ideas I can't relate to.

—Kerry, Brighton, UK

C IS FOR CURIOUS

Curious, or questioning, as is often now used, means just that—someone who is in the process of asking the big questions. I think all young people should spend time thinking about desire. I think everyone would be a lot happier if they took a few weeks to dwell on what does it for them. It'd resolve a lot of tension and grief, I expect. A whole lot of people "experiment"—they give it a little go to see if they like it. Some do, and do it again, and some rule it out, happy in the knowledge that they're not missing out.

Like anything in life, sometimes you don't know until you try. I wouldn't eat prawns until I was eighteen—the mere idea of them freaked me out. But then I tried them and it turns out they're DELISH. Don't worry, I've more than made up for it since.

(I stress, in this instance, that "prawns" is not a euphemism for anything.)

A IS FOR ASEXUAL

There are two ways of looking at asexuality. The first is as a lack of, or little interest in, sex (with anyone). The second is as a refusal to define your sexual orientation or uncertainty about your sexual orientation—a more modern use of the term.

Asexuality is not celibacy (abstaining from sex). Asexual people MAY have sex—to have kids, to try it out, or to experiment—but asexual people will characteristically have little desire for either men or women, so if you go back to our flow chart, they would typically lose interest after the first question.

Asexual people will often have romantic feelings toward people, and they may well have boyfriends and girlfriends and do all the lovey-dovey, holding hands and hugging parts, just without the weenies and va-jay-jays.

Aromantic is similar to asexual. You can probably figure out this one with no help from me. Aromantic peeps may well feel platonic love for their friends or families but have little or no interest in forming romantic relationships.

This is—you guessed it—FINE. Some people just aren't that sexual and, like all identities, this one might change over time. I have found that a growing number of teenagers identify as asexual while figuring out their identity.

T IS FOR TRANSGENDER

Right at the very outset of this discussion, let's not get it twisted.

Here we go:

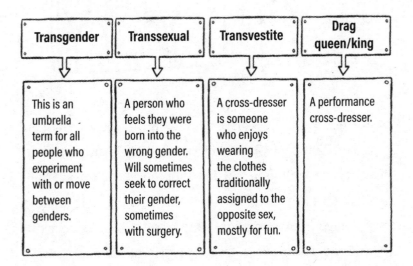

Transgender	Transsexual	Transvestite	Drag queen/king
This is an umbrella term for all people who experiment with or move between genders.	A person who feels they were born into the wrong gender. Will sometimes seek to correct their gender, sometimes with surgery.	A cross-dresser is someone who enjoys wearing the clothes traditionally assigned to the opposite sex, mostly for fun.	A performance cross-dresser.

Now this is really tough, and you'd be forgiven for making mistakes when "trans" is so often used as shorthand. When it is, it almost always means transgender or transsexual. You may also hear **genderqueer**, which, like queer theory regarding sexuality, is more of a refusal to be pigeonholed than an identity in itself.

Using "trans" as an umbrella term causes one big problem. Some misinformed people think that all trans people have had some form of surgery to "correct" their gender. This is a hangover from the outdated terminology "sex change." Trans people *may* have had surgery or be taking medication, but many won't have had either of those things.

As with "dyke," you absolutely don't have permission to use the word "tranny" unless you, yourself, are transgender. Got that? Good.

There are broader issues regarding gender identity, in that we are still very much stuck in a binary culture which says some things are for boys (slugs and snails and puppy dogs' tails) and some things are for girls (sugar and spice and all things nice—P.S. Who wrote this ANTIFEMINIST HATE ANTHEM? To think we tell it to children in NURSERY SCHOOL).

Advertisers would like us to believe that being female somehow feels different to being male, but we will never really know.

Culture tells our parents how to dress us as kids, and it becomes ingrained. It sometimes seems bonkers to me to think that a dude would have to be "trans" to put on a skirt or some heels. Who bloody says that they are "female attire"? Sadly, as most of the world is blind to how small-minded this is, that's the way the cookie crumbles. For now.

As we said in the last chapter, although the studies of gender and sexuality are closely linked, they are largely unrelated: A person will choose separate identities for both. For instance, I used to identify as a gay man. Now, I'm a straight trans woman. You see?

RORY'S STORY

Rory from Brighton identifies as a trans man. He had surgery and took hormones to change gender several years ago. Here is his story:

> I always liked to dress up and be the boy. At primary school, everyone knew me as "the girl who wanted to be a boy." The other kids used to tease me about it on the playground, and it would make me cry, but I didn't know why I was upset by it. Maybe it was the singling out?
>
> So I'd get taken aside by my teacher. I couldn't understand what the big deal was; who wouldn't want to be a boy?
>
> As an adult, I found a way of being a boy that was acceptable and adored. I was Rory Raven, drag king extraordinaire! For years I had been dressing up in private, wearing very masculine clothes—shirts with a tie, suits, suspenders, a trilby hat. But I felt I had to hide, that there was something wrong with it. I'd even have to get changed back into my normal clothes just to use the bathroom in my own home, just in case my flatmates saw me. But as a drag king I would be on stage wearing the clothes publicly that I felt comfortable wearing. At the end of the performances, I'd watch my fellow drag kings remove their drag and change into their regular clothes. They'd

scrub off the fake facial hair and five o'clock shadow and replace it instead with makeup—lipstick and eyeshadow, feminine and understated. I wanted to stay in my drag and felt at a loss when the evening was over.

For my twenty-fourth birthday I was given a binder. A binder is a tight-fitting vest which is worn underneath clothes that makes the wearer look flat-chested and, therefore, male. It was tight and uncomfortable, and wearing it wasn't pleasant. Getting into it wasn't easy. Getting out was even harder. I thought I was going to accidentally suffocate myself trying to take the thing off for the first time. But wearing it gave me such liberation. I felt like I was being seen for the first time. So I kept wearing it, even when I wasn't performing.

Soon enough, I began to wonder: What's the difference between Rory onstage and Rory in real life? My friends were already calling me Rory as a nickname, and some of them were even referring to me with male pronouns.

I decided to take off the fake beard and just start living full-time as Rory (only without the ornithological surname). Work was really supportive. I know I was lucky in this regard, as I worked for a trans charity at the time. They didn't bat an eyelid.

My name change was the most important part of my transition. Choosing my name was a profound and powerful decision. It would be a mixture of who I was and who I wanted to be. The timing of my legal change was important too. It was a few days before my twenty-fifth birthday, which, for me, is the start of my new year, and coincidently was the beginning of the new year for several religions and cultures worldwide.

Life has paradoxically [become] both better and a lot harder since transition. Coming out to everyone is an ongoing process. Some friends could see it coming, so were unfazed; others took a bit longer and, sadly, I have lost contact with some people altogether. My adopted queer family [has] embraced me, and that has given me a lot of strength. Transition has opened doors I didn't know existed, and I have made a lot of new friends along the way.

Helping trans friends: A lot of people struggle with the pronoun game. This is understandable; after all, for years and years you've used, i.e., "he" to describe your friend and now she is asking to be called "she." It can take time to adjust. However, you should always respect your friend's choice. If you think it's hard, how hard do you think it is for your friend? Get on board with a new pronoun quickly and never EVER use the word "it" or "he/she." That is NOT COOL.

N IS FOR NONBINARY

Increasingly, people are rejecting traditional concepts of male and female. Perhaps we're *all* waking up to the idea that gender, largely, is a construct. Yes, some people think we are wholly defined by our biology and genes, but I think that steers us into some very bleak territory. As Chaz Bono once said, "Gender is between your ears, not your legs," and that's so true. As we can't know if being male *feels* one way and being female *feels* different (as we only have our individual experience to go on), all we can ever control is how we wish to express our personal identities. For some people, that's traditionally female, for some it's traditionally male, but for many, many people it's *neither* or *both*. Guess what? That's fine. "Nonbinary" or "genderfluid" are becoming identities in their own right and free people up to express their gender however they like. Miley Cyrus described herself as gender-fluid in 2015, raising awareness further. In 2019, singer Sam Smith came out as nonbinary and uses they/them pronouns.

In places, I've used MTF (male-to-female) and FTM (female-to-male) to describe binary transgender people. For nonbinary people, obviously, this won't quite apply. That said, hospitals, doctors, and scientists still use these terms, so I felt I needed to in places as well. Rest assured though, a nonbinary or genderqueer person's experience of gender is every bit as valid as mine.

INTERSEX

Intersex is not so much an identity, in that you can't really choose it. (Remember, you can't choose your preference, but you can choose a label or identity.) Since intersex is used as a label, by both intersex people and doctors, it's worth mentioning here. A person is born intersex if they have genitalia or sexual characteristics that do not conform to strict definitions of male and/or female. This does NOT make them transgender, as they may agree with the gender they are assigned (most intersex people, rightly or wrongly, are assigned a sex at birth).

Transgender issues are linked with intersex issues, as many intersex people grow up to disagree with the gender they were assigned and seek to change.

WHAT IS CISGENDER?

Cisgender is basically the opposite of transgender. It simply means when your gender identity matches the identity you were given at birth. Therefore, the majority of people will identify as "cis" even if they don't know it—it removes the need for anyone to say they are "normal," which, as we said, is an unpleasant word.

As a final word on all these identities, gay-rights activist Peter Tatchell says he looks forward to a day when all of these labels will be redundant and we can all just be human. I think I look forward to that day too.

However you identify, be it lesbian, gay, bisexual, trans, queer, asexual, curious, or carrot, we all have something in common—we are a minority, and we have made brave steps to identify as such; we have refused to hide and made a declaration of who we are. So label shop, label swap, or don't wear one at all. Just be comfortable with YOU and let others wear whatever labels they like.

This first step, our self-acceptance, is by FAR the hardest step of the journey. The rest, this book can help with.

If you identify as straight, you should keep reading too. Frankly, LGBTQ+ people need all the straight allies we can get, and you too can arm yourself with knowledge.

CHAPTER 3

YOU CAN'T MISTAKE OUR BIOLOGY

How old were you when you realized "being gay" was a thing? Probably pretty young...five? Six? Seven? Now, how old were you when you asked the bigger question of WHY people are gay? There has to be a reason.

Before we examine some of the possible factors that made you who you are, I think it's important to state that IT DOESN'T MATTER. We don't need excuses for our existence, and I don't hear anyone asking heterosexual people, "What made you straight?"

Remember High Priestess Gaga and "Born This Way." Your sexuality or gender is as natural as your eye color, and you should never be ashamed of it.

WARNING: This section is jam-packed with enough GOBBLEDYGOOK to stretch my pitiful biology KNOWLEDGE to its breaking point. Get a cup of tea and prepare for some SCIENCE.

So what made us same-sex inclined or transgender? Well, don't hold your breath, because I'm afraid the experts at the RuPaul Institute of Gay Heritage Technology (RIGHT) really can't come to anything resembling a definitive answer—more a collection of half-convincing theories.

Let's take a look at the most coherent, starting with sexuality.

1. Twin Studies

Several studies have been carried out to show that identical twins have a much higher chance of BOTH being gay than nonidentical twins, suggesting that there is some sort of "gay gene." However, it is thought that gay twins are keen to volunteer for scientific studies, and this may have somewhat skewed the data.

2. Chromosome Linkage

In the 1990s, there were various studies on the catchily named chromosome Xq28—the so-called "gay gene." In GAY MEN, this gene is passed down on the mother's side of the family, often seeming to explain why gay men may have gay brothers or gay uncles.

3. Epigenetics

Oh, it's only going to get more complicated, I'm afraid. After work surrounding Xq28 was somewhat discredited, scientists instead looked to "epi-marks" as a possible explanation. I want you to imagine your mom's and dad's genetic codes (don't worry, I'm not going to ask you to imagine them bumping uglies). On some of our genes, we have epi-marks. These are sort of like Post-it Notes with added information for the gene's job. On the male chromosomes, it may have "YO—YOU SHOULD LIKE GIRLS" written on it, while the female chromosomes may come with a note saying, "YOU DEFINITELY WANT TO HAVE SEX WITH DUDES." Now, for a long time it was assumed that these Post-its were removed before being passed via SWEATY PARENT SEX (sorry, couldn't resist) to their baby. But now scientists believe this isn't always the case and that sometimes these Post-it Notes saying whom you're meant to fancy get "stuck" onto the kids. So, in short, boys can get the epi-mark for liking boys from their moms, and girls can get the epi-mark for liking girls from their dads.

Tell them that they should freak out about your sexuality. I imagine they'll enjoy being blamed.

4. More Science-y Theories

Having lots of brothers—With each boy baby, your mom's

immune system gets better at blocking male hormones in the womb, making gay male babies more likely. (Note how a lot of studies have focused on gay men. Figures. The patriarchy.)

Pheromones—An area of men's (again men, I'm afraid) brains reacts differently to different scents depending on sexuality. Gay men's brains respond to locker-room sweat smell, while straight men respond to a compound found in lady pee. Humans are gross.

Brain structure—Several studies have found that the hypothalamus part of the brain may be a little different in homosexual people. That said, they found this for the most part through poking about in sheep.

Prenatal hormones—Linked to the "having lots of brothers" idea, this is the idea that the changes in brain structure possibly come from the levels of androgen that we are exposed to in the womb—it can change the "gender" of our brain, including sexual attraction. Oh, OK.

EXOTIC BECOMES EROTIC

I like this one for no other reason than that it has a silly name. This idea states that our biology (brains, hormones, genes) predisposes us to like stuff associated with one gender more than the other. Eventually, we see those who are exotic (i.e., boys if we like girl stuff, girls if we're typically more masculine) as sexy.

I'm meant to be an impartial reporter of these theories, but this one seems like total ass. I mean, REALLY?

EVOLUTIONARY STUDIES

Clearly, there are some issues with the idea of a "gay gene." Gay men and lesbians who had babies would produce gay babies, right? Wrong. Why are there so many gay people coming from straight parents?

From a Darwinian perspective, homosexuality makes no sense—if we were all gay, the human race would die out. Gay people (being less likely to now reproduce) remove themselves from the gene pool.

There have been several theories about this. One is that perhaps the gene predisposing people to homosexuality actually poses a benefit in heterosexual people (only sometimes making the person LGBTQ+), and this is why the trait continues to be passed down through generations. Another theory is that gay uncles and aunts tend to dote more on their nieces or nephews, helping to ensure the youngsters' survival and in that way propagating their own genetic code.

BIOLOGICAL DIFFERENCES

- Gay men and straight women have equally proportioned brain hemispheres. Gay women and straight men have slightly larger right hemispheres.
- Gay men have slightly longer and thicker winkies. **Excellent.**
- The amygdala of gay men is more responsive to porn than those of straight men. So we have bigger dicks and we're hornier. Jus' sayin'.
- Finger-length ratios may vary between lesbians and straight women. Get combing the streets with a finger ruler, ladies!

A PROBLEM I HAVE

All of these theories seem to have us programmed to be GAY or STRAIGHT from before we were born. I find this very exclusive of bi, curious, and queer people.

Clearly, biology is playing into our sexual preference—but not our lifestyle choices. No gene is going to help you come out, nor is it going to determine what kind of family situation you're born into. Therefore, environmental factors must play a huge role that shouldn't be overlooked.

I imagine a child born into a liberal, accepting family in the U.S. is far more likely to IDENTIFY as gay or lesbian than a child born into a strict Muslim family in Yemen. You get me?

Also, I doubt there's a gene for "bored and horny" or "feeling a bit experimental." I worry that scientists don't take into account the fluidity or playfulness of sex and sexuality. My advice is to be interested and go "Mmmm" when reading the theories in this chapter but to simply accept that when it comes to sexuality, IT IS HOW IT IS. And that's fine. Enjoy!

BIOLOGICAL EXPLANATIONS

For many decades, it was thought that being trans was a result of environmental or parental factors. However, the high-profile case of David Reimer (1965–2004) changed things somewhat. Born as a boy and called "Bruce," Reimer was accidentally castrated in a botched circumcision and was raised as a girl. However, David ALWAYS identified as male, suggesting gender cannot be learned—our identity is born with us.

Modern scientists have found possible genetic causes for transgenderism: Both male-to-female (MTF) and female-to-male (FTM) transsexuals have variations in hormone-binding genes, while FTM transsexuals may also be lacking some female-only gene distribution patterns.

Other scientists have found variations in brain structure in both MTF and FTM transsexuals—in both cases, the test subjects have the typical brain patterns of their preferred gender identity.

Finally, and this is AMAZING, FTM transsexuals often report "phantom limb syndrome" for a penis from childhood, and while cis men who have lost their members DO get phantom penis sensations, MTF patients do NOT. Mind-blowing stuff, right? GHOST WEINERS. (There's my next YA book.) As with sexuality, I'm not big into biological determinism. We are all free to play with gender.

WHAT HAVE WE LEARNED?

OK, that was a whole lot of science. I hope you feel cleverer; I certainly do. I have summarized about a hundred experiments and studies over the previous few pages. There are tons and tons of research papers and books you can track down if you want more information on this—it is fascinating.

I think the important thing to take away from this chapter is that we have little control over our sexual desires or gender even if we do have control over our identity. However you choose to identify, though, no one can ever say your feelings are a choice. I'll say it again: When it comes to who you fancy or who you are, IT IS HOW IT IS and you never, ever have to apologize for this. You were born this way.

THINGS THAT DID NOT MAKE YOU GAY

CHAPTER 4

STEREOTYPES
ARE POO

Aren't gay men AMAZING? They are such loyal friends and they're always good for a laugh. They're the BEST shopping partners too and are always up for dancing to Beyoncé!

GBFs 4EVA!

Yes, dear, and all Irish people are leprechauns and Paris is full of onion-wearing mime artists.

Representation of LGBTQ+ people in the media is getting BETTER, but it is still vastly limited. Unless you are one of the lucky people who grew up around gay people, you might think that all gay men are fabulously campy talk show hosts and all gay women are sports commentators. Hopefully, you recognize that this isn't the case. You can probably count the number of transgender people on TV on one hand.

LEGENDARY gay rights campaigner Harvey Milk encouraged all gay people to be more visible so that young people would be surrounded by a spectrum of infinitely varied gay people—that way people would see that stereotypes are meaningless.

Let's take a look at some common stereotypes about gay people.

Stereotype	Fact or Fiction?
All gay men dress like gods and dance like Fred Astaire.	Go to any gay club on a Saturday night and you'll see a sublime mixture of dad dancing, self-conscious shuffling, and over-the-top arms-aloft raving. Some gay men dress well, and some dress like David Hasselhoff.
All gay women have short hair.	Yes. Gay women have a faulty version of the hair-growing gene. What do you think? Of course this isn't true! Lots of gay women have long hair, and straight women have short hair.
Gay men are pedophiles.	Ah, this old chestnut. Some deeply homophobic people truly believe this is the case. Think about it—you know what gay men like? BIG, HAIRY MEN. You know who have none of these attributes? Kids. Gay men like men—that's the whole point.
Gay men always work as flight attendants or hairdressers.	Some do. Most don't.
Gay women hate men.	I imagine they'd hate men who said that to them, yes.
Gay women are all desperate to have threesomes with men, just like in porn.	This feeds into the age-old misconception that all gay people are waiting for is the "right guy/girl" to make them realize the error of their ways.
Gay men are massive sluts.	Firstly, we don't use that word because it's not very nice. We'll discuss this in much more detail later, but CLEARLY this isn't true of all gay men.

All trans people are gay.	TWO DIFFERENT THINGS. If you draw a little Venn diagram, there will be a bit in the middle where the gay circle overlaps the trans circle, but that's true of anything, right?
Gay men all have HIV/AIDS.	Le sigh. Sadly, this is why a lot of older people are wary of gay men. This statement is WRONG on about fifty levels, all of which are potentially dangerous. We will discuss the AIDS pandemic and STIs in much more detail later because they ARE important to gay culture.
Gay women all have cats.	Yes. All of them. It's how they plan to conquer the world. A platoon of lesbians with armored cats. *Sarcastic face*
Gay men are "girls."	Gay men are, in fact, men.
Bisexual people are "hedging their bets."	If this were the case, wouldn't we ALL do it?
Transsexual people are cross-dressers.	We discussed this in the section on being trans.
Transgender people are sick.	Sick to death of statements like that, yes.
Trans people pose a threat in public bathrooms.	There are **no** recorded cases of transgender people attacking **anyone** in public bathrooms. In fact, trans people are much more frequently **victims** of harassment and violence in restrooms.

I think you get the message—there are far, far too many stereotypes about LGBTQ+ people.

WHY STEREOTYPES ARE POO

> I think all stereotypes are sh*t. Whether it's a racial stereotype or a sexual stereotype or a cultural stereotype, you're always going to find SOMEONE who fits the bill. But stereotypes suggest that a group, or at least a majority of that group, behaves in a certain way, and that kills the idea of individuality.
>
> —BFL, 43, Minnesota

Stereotypes are useless for one very simple reason—they dehumanize people and allow terrible prejudices and discrimination to come creeping in. Bigots THRIVE on stereotypes. It's much easier to hate a faceless stereotype than it is a human being.

As well as being awesome, LGBTQ+ people are also a persecuted minority. This is not awesome. I'm afraid it's not all cocktail parties and gay cruises—for many people all around the world, being gay is ILLEGAL. I know, it's cray.

The treatment of transgender people in the U.S. media

is especially worrisome. There are so many debates about the "threat" that transgender people pose to "women and children" even though there is no evidence to suggest such a threat exists. Nonetheless, the mysterious threat has been discussed so often, people have started to believe there is one.

Similarly, stereotypes about LGBTQ+ people fuel homophobia, which we will talk about a lot more in the next chapter.

Each LGBTQ+ person is completely unique and individual. Although a lot of gay people might like some of the same things (there is a rich and varied gay or queer culture), no two LGBTQ+ people are the same.

Even if you identify as gay, lesbian, bisexual, transgender, or queer, you're still just you. There are infinite ways of being gay, and they're all brilliant. So saying things like, "All gay men dress well," is unhelpful and dehumanizing to the gay men who don't give a flying fig about fashion.

Remember, being gay is just one element of your identity, so how could we possibly all be the same?

WHICH STEREOTYPES BUG YOU?

I find the "gay best friend" stereotype very grating.

—R, 17, London, UK

Lesbians as man-haters; bisexuals as promiscuous and/ or secretly preferring men, or not existing; asexuals being nonexistent; and all asexual people being prudes.

—Nina, 16, UK

Stereotypes that all gay men are super feminine and all lesbians are super masculine are annoying. In high school, there were a lot of rumors that I was a lesbian (which I was pretty okay with, honestly), because of my short hair, disinterest in boys, and refusal to follow fashion trends.

—Chris, 18, New York

All gay men are promiscuous, bisexuals of all genders are promiscuous, black lesbians are always butch and aggressive, and feminine lesbians are bisexual really; trans people all have issues.

—Mica, 23, London, UK

The stereotype that bisexual people are only looking for sex, and that when/if they get married, they are "choosing" one gender over the other.

—Claire, 15, Oregon

Lesbians as butch or masculine. Like all people, we come in all shapes, sizes, ways of dress, etc. I hate being told that I can't be gay because I don't "look like a lesbian." Another one that gets me is that lesbians are good at fixing things, 'cause I sure as hell ain't!

—Michelle, 23, U.S.

The one that really bothers me is the assumption that all MTF trans people are perverts, transitioning to gain some kind of sexual thrill from their position.

—Laura, 21, UK

SUBCULTURES VS. STEREOTYPES

Every once in a blue moon, stereotypes may have the tiniest grain of truth (lots of gay men DO like Beyoncé, but who doesn't? She's the dancing Aslan of pop), but that doesn't mean it should be applied to a whole group! Except for the one about Parisian mimes. That's all true. KIDDING!

One of the best things about choosing to IDENTIFY as gay or bi is that you are already making your own rules. I'm not for a second suggesting there is one set of rules for straight people and one for nonstraight, but identifying as LGBTQ+ means you have opted out of the majority group (you're never too young to learn that the whole world is largely run and designed for straight, white, cis men, or "the patriarchy"). This pretty much means you are free to adopt whichever elements of gay or queer culture you see fit.

The biggest bonus to coming out is that you can be who you want to be with no hiding and no apologies.

> [When I came out] it was easier, because I had been pretending to be something I wasn't. Being gay meant that I could be more honest about the things that I liked.
> —Ben, 23, Manchester, UK

Basically, you can pick and choose which "stereotypes" you want to adhere to, because some of them are part of a great tradition set out by generations of LGBTQ+ people. What if you DO want to work as a flight attendant? Do it. What if you want to work as a flight attendant AND play rugby AND listen to musical theatre soundtracks BUT ALSO thrash metal? Well, guess what? Your identity is yours to design.

If you're a gay girl who wants to shave her head, who the heck has any right to tell you not to? It's your hair.

I'd like to point out that LGBTQ+ people do not cause homophobia or transphobia simply by being. Homophobes and transphobes are simply bigoted, and that, my friend, is their problem.

LGBTQ+ people do not choose to be LGBTQ+. Bigots choose to hate.

There are various threads to gay culture which are not stereotypes, but are rather identities within an identity. You can't choose whether you fancy guys or girls, but once you've accepted who you like, there ARE lifestyle choices to be made. These are some of the various subcultures you may have heard about or may experience on the gay scene:

BEARS
This refers to big, hairy gay men, often with beards.

CUBS
Not surprisingly, these are YOUNGER big, hairy gay men, often with beards.

OTTERS

SLIMMER hairy guys with beards.
I'm not making this up, seriously.

BUTCH DYKE

This refers to a gay woman who has
adopted some traditionally male
characteristics (e.g., a mustache) but
doesn't identify as male. Remember,
it's only OK to use the term "dyke"
if you're describing yourself.

TWINKS

This one is for the boys again. A
twink is usually a young, hairless
gay man. Waxing strips at the ready!

SCALLIES

Usually a gay guy with a penchant
for sportswear and man jewelry.

MUSCLE MARY

A muscular gay man. Body
worship and gay men are closely
linked. More on this later.

FEM/LIPSTICK LESBIAN

A gay woman who enjoys
"traditionally female" dress,
hair, and makeup (although
what does THAT mean?).

Of course, most gay men and women are NONE of those things and are just men or women who are into people with the same gender as them. It's an identity buffet—you can take your plate up and just have a little scoop of gay, or you can go nuts and load up on as many labels as you can carry back to the table.

> I sometimes think it would be easier if I did look more like a stereotypical "lesbian," because it would be easier to [attract dates]! But that's just not me...you have to wear the clothes you like.
>
> —Jenny, 31, Dublin, Ireland

If you identify as lesbian or gay, I bet you think you're pretty good at being able to spot a fellow 'mo, right? I'd like you to take a pen and in the space at right draw a gay man and a gay woman...GO!

I bet some of you have drawn either:

But for many decades, LGBTQ+ people had to be INVISIBLE for fear of persecution. Therefore, most gay men and women had to blend in effortlessly, like alien bodysnatchers—only not evil, obviously. It's super homophobic to suggest that all gay men and women look alike.

That said, some gay men and women enjoy playing with style and gender typing. Any subculture will have uniforms to an extent—look at goths or mods, etc. Adopting a certain sexual-identity look is very different to being transgender, as we discussed in the section on identity. It is more about an aesthetic—borrowing gender norms or aspiring toward androgyny. Why shouldn't a woman cut her hair short? Why shouldn't guys wear makeup? Part of the fun of being LGBTQ+ is giving the finger to "the norm."

In the next section, let's look at some particular stereotypes, starting with gay men.

CAMP

The word "camp" is often applied to gay men, although anything can be camp. Gay women can be fantastically camp—just look at Michelle Visage. Camp means excessive, flamboyant, kitsch, and theatrical but also sophisticated, witty, and subversive behavior or things. Later on, when we look at "gay icons," you'll see that many celebrities beloved by gay people possess these qualities.

Despite "camp" sounding literally fabulous, it is more often than not used as an insult, sometimes by straight people but, perhaps more shockingly, by gay people themselves. "He's too campy for me" trips off the tongue of many a gay guy when he's deciding whether or not to get with someone.

Another term we could have added to the definition of camp is "effeminate," and this is where the problem seems to be.

It seems unlikely that young gay men are born camp, and yet, when I was a teacher, there were glaringly camp five- and six-year-olds in my Year 1 classes. How can this be? One possibility is that these "boys" actually identify as female from a young age—lots of trans people do (remember Rory's story). Another theory is that young gay men have a refined eye for camp and track down camp icons in the media and emulate their behavior. Whatever the origin of camp, it's fair to say that however butch gay men think they are, total strangers are often MORE than able to spot a gay chap at twenty paces, especially if they themselves are gay.

If we were to ask a hundred gay men, "Do you think you're camp?" though, they'd scratch their testicles, adopt a tone ten decibels lower than normal, and say, "Naaaarrr, mate, not me." I estimate possibly three or four might say, "Oooh, sometimes, if I've had a drink."

Is this simply roaring misogyny? Do gay men just hate

women and anything stereotypically female? Living in a male-dominated world seems to have infected us with a notion that anything male is BETTER. Is this why some gay women ALSO reject feminine norms and chase down the characteristics of the dominant group on the planet—men?

Being gay doesn't make you immune to misogyny, but I think it's more than that. After DECADES of being told in all sorts of ways that gay men are LESS THAN straight men, the community has turned that hate inward. We aren't rejecting female traits; we're rejecting stereotypically gay ones.

How sad is this? Answer: mega sad. Because being gay or lesbian is FABULOUS. It is GLORIOUS.

So we might not all like all of our stereotypes, but they are ours. They belong to us. The rest of the world is so shady about gay people that, love it or hate it, I think we could all be a little bit more supportive of gay culture. Let me tell you something, we can 'straight act' all we want, but if you're sleeping with your own sex, to the rest of the world you're as gay as John Waters living in a pink tent with Rachel Maddow while watching *Drag Race*.

The same could be said of trans people who denounce the trans label or "live stealth." While I only ever set out to be a woman, I am still very open about my journey. It's nothing to be ashamed of. If people think I'm a freak, good, I certainly wouldn't want to be like them: mean. You might as well celebrate it. And *this* is part of the reason why we call our celebrations *Pride*.

DESPERATE DANS

As mentioned previously, any subculture may develop a uniform, but for some gay men the "look" has gone far beyond mere clothing. It's—you guessed it—a stereotype, but gay men are often thought to have the best bodies on Instagram.

Go to any big gay club and—another stereotype incoming—you'll see HUGE guys, arms aloft, with their tops off. Barrel chests, six-packs, and necks as big as my thigh have become the norm. It seems the aspirational aesthetic is that of CARTOON HUMAN Desperate Dan.

Gym culture is now just...culture. Look at *Love Island*! Men are more body conscious than ever before. There's a lot of pressure on all young men, but young *gay* men are more likely to be naked around *other* men. Double the pressure. This pressure may have real consequences. Gay and bisexual men and boys are significantly more likely to suffer from eating disorders than their straight counter-parts (Feldman & Meyer 2007).

The Velvet Rage author Alan Downs posits that the gay obsession with body mass is down to self-loathing. He believes gay men chase impossible levels of fitness to overcome an inner sadness—you'll be happy if only you become that bit more perfect. He believes gay men look for validation in all the wrong places.

We are subjected to peer pressure, even as adults—we see very muscular bodies in porn, in the club, on the beach and we think it's easily achievable. This is something that women have been subjected to for years, particularly from exposure to six-foot, ninety-pound models in fashion magazines.

Some guys are going to extreme lengths to fit in down the clubs. Given that I've never seen a straight guy dancing with his shirt off, it's not a mystery to figure out why.

Know this: A six-pack never made anyone happy. No one ever got to the stage at the gym where they said, "I DID IT! I AM NOW SATISFIED."

We can all do our part to make the gay community nicer, kinder, and more body positive. Follow a diverse bunch of people on social media: do follow traditionally hunky guys, but ALSO follow trans men; skinny guys; thicc and juicy guys; guys with disabilities.

Everybody and every body is beautiful.

STEROIDS

Desperate Dan bodies are also no great enigma. STEROIDS. I'm afraid it's that simple. Go to a gay beach and play REAL

OR STEROIDS? Some guys have naturally lean, defined, or even muscled bodies, but I think you can spot a steroid user a mile off. Steroid use is endemic on the gay scene. All those really huge guys, with few exceptions, are using.

So. Let's talk about the 'roids. The ones we're talking about are anabolic-androgenic steroids (or AAS for short). Users inject or swallow high doses of the male hormone testosterone, which promotes growth. Most users take them noncontinuously, causing fluctuations in their body mass as and when they need to look buff. Some users take a cocktail of different steroids, a practice known as "stacking."

If everyone's on them, they can't be so bad, right? Right? Wrong.

BENEFITS	For the duration you take the hormone, you will get bigger, especially if usage is combined with a stringent gym routine.
SIDE EFFECTS	**Mental/Behavioral:** Aggression · Mood swings · Paranoia · Mania · Delusions · Depression · Suicidal thoughts · Reduced sex drive · Insomnia **Physical:** Enlarging of the heart · Heart attack · Liver damage · Severe acne · Fluid retention · Testicular shrinkage · Low sperm count · Baldness · Increased risk of prostate cancer · Risk of HIV and hepatitis through needle use

I think that table speaks for itself. As with any illegal drug (note that some people are prescribed hormone treatment for valid reasons), **just because your friends are doing it doesn't mean it's safe.**

Also, I'm not sure how I can say this delicately. NO ONE WANTS TO HAVE SEX WITH A BALD SPOTTY PSYCHO WITH BALLS LIKE SHRIVELED RAISINS. (I'm known for my tact.)

So it's a vicious circle. Guys will only look buff for as long as they're on the drugs, so you are well aware your physique is not because of your genes or your efforts at the gym—like fake self-esteem. Frankly, it's cheating, pure and simple.

More to the point, no one ever made themselves happy just by going to the gym. The big guys still wanna be bigger. It's a never-ending quest for a state of perfection that doesn't exist. Guys on steroids aren't happier; they're just bigger. Finally, the Desperate Dan look is very specific, and not everyone is into that 'roidy look. It's no guarantee of finding a love match.

> You can tell when a guy's on steroids—bulging head veins! I personally think it's not such a great look. Huge, great arms and chests with skinny little legs. I find it repulsive, to be honest.
>
> —T, 22, Brisbane, Australia

GIRL WARS

While gay men wage war against camp with muscle, gay women have their own infights. This war is about femininity. "Butch dykes" often take issue with "lipstick lesbians" and vice versa. You hear a lot of arguments like this:

"I'm a lesbian so I want a woman who actually looks like a woman." Or "She's just pretending to be femme; she's really a dyke."

As with gay men, this infighting isn't helping anyone—we get enough grief from outside the community as it is. It seems that some women feel that adhering to or avoiding stereotypes is somehow damaging "the cause," but of course this isn't true. All any person can be is comfortable. It's all about personal taste.

Some women like makeup and fashion, and some don't.

You'll notice that THIS HAS NOTHING TO DO WITH SEXUALITY. In fact, what is more troubling is that straight women might be accused of being gay purely because they don't like fussing over their hair, clothes, and makeup—that's both homophobic AND sexist.

What's more, when it comes to dating, some women are very into butch lesbians, some women are into girly girls—there really is something for everyone.

MAN-HATERS

A mixture of poor media representation and sheer misogyny has also furthered the myth of the "angry lesbian," the idea that all gay women are militants who seek to kill and scalp men. This response is identical to the one that women get from men when they use the word "feminism." It's a way of men putting women down—to keep them in their place. Note that feminists are often accused of being lesbians. Let's get it straight. Gay women do not hate men. They simply don't want to have sex with them.

Very often, when talking about women's issues, I find the term "men" is used to describe "the patriarchy." This is also a mistake.

"JOIN US"

This is so ridiculous it hardly warrants airtime, but pornography (more on that later) has led some young heterosexual men to think that scantily clad gay women will coquettishly beckon them into a soft-focus three-way. Clearly this is not the case.

Some bi or queer women probably are looking for threesomes with clammy-palmed Internet men, but most aren't. No lesbian women are. I can't state this enough: Lesbians like vaginas.

They don't even want blokes watching. I KNOW, how INCONSIDERATE. Note the sarcastic tone.

There is a more serious side to the idea that gay women are "waiting for the right man." In certain parts of South Africa, "corrective rape" is a terrible, heartbreaking practice whereby gay women (as many as an estimated ten a week) are raped or gang-raped "for their own good" to turn them heterosexual. All of us, straight, gay, or otherwise must, MUST accept that women of all sexualities have the same sexual freedoms as men.

GAY VS. LESBIAN

One of the strangest stereotypes about us is that gay men hate lesbians and vice versa. Imma save you some time. If you are chatting to gay men who are dismissive of lesbians (or for that matter disparaging of the vagina as a concept), you are talking to misogynist dicks. If you are talking to a gay woman who classifies all gay men as lesbian haters, you are talking to a sexist homophobe.

It works both ways.

Needless to say, gay people often show a startling lack of awareness about trans people—confusing drag queens and transgender people constantly.

There is no reason for these conflicts, beyond trashy,

worn, flea-bitten, drag-show stand-up jokes that should have been thrown out with crimpers and Tamagotchis.

Again, there is so much homophobia in the world. Why on earth would we want to add to it?

OUT IN THE COLD

Poor bisexual people. I'll include queer, pan, and curious people in this section too. Because as humans we're trained to enjoy binary things, people not conforming to GAY OR STRAIGHT can often be rejected by both sides.

Straight people think bisexuals are "greedy" or "indecisive," while gay people lean toward, "Oh they must be gay." Both think that, "when they meet the right person, they'll pick a team." As I said before, I really don't think bisexual people would bother hedging their bets. It would be so much EASIER to pick a side, I'd imagine. Therefore, it takes guts to identify this way.

It's up to you to decide if bi people are getting the best or worst of both worlds. I'd argue that bisexual people aren't getting any of the privileges of straight society while they're also lacking the community of being gay or lesbian.

Let's all hug a bisexual this week. They need our support too.

GENDER STUDIES

Given that most homophobia stems from misogyny (mocking boys for "acting like girls" and girls for "acting like boys") I find it enormously frustrating that LGBTQ+ people enter into it.

Misogyny amongst gay and bi men takes the form of making fun of female genitalia ("Ew! Gross! Vagina!", "serving fish", etc). For some gay and bi women, misandry is the aforementioned "man-hating" or "all men are rapists" attitude.

But *both* have it in for trans people. Mocking trans people as "chicks with dicks" or "they're not *real* men/women" and such undermines the entire trans experience—an experience cisgender people will never fully understand. It's hugely indecent to ask trans people about their genitals or "the op." Trans people are NOT defined by what's between their legs.

It gets worse. Nonbinary people are widely mocked by straight, cis, and LGBTQ+ people alike. The "OH, I IDENTIFY AS A HELICOPTER" brigade. The terminology may be newish, but gender-nonconforming people have been around forever. There's a special place in Hades for trans people who criticize nonbinary folks for not following the traditional medical transition.

CONFORMITY

In any group, there are bound to be social norms, and being LGBTQ+ is no different. Perhaps some stereotypes arose from these shared attributes. No one has to conform to these traits, however. Despite the hundreds of stereotypes we've talked about in this chapter—regarding hairstyles, clothes, behavior—it's important to remember that even if you DO conform to certain stereotypes, you are still an individual. There is only one you, and you can do whatever you like as long as you look after yourself and don't hurt anyone else.

Who do you want to be? There's only one rule: Always be true to yourself.

CHAPTER 5
THE FEAR

So far, I hope I've sold this LGBTQ+ thing pretty well. I mean, it does sound brilliant, doesn't it? You get to dress how you like and make out with whomever you want. It's hip and trendy. You get to be part of an avant-garde subculture with links to art, music, and fashion. But, most importantly, you will be at one with who you really are. You are finally you.

HURRAH!

Ah, if only it were that simple. While some people glide effortlessly out of the closet like prize figure skaters, others find the process more akin to Bambi learning to walk. For some, coming to terms with their sexuality and coming out is the hardest thing they will ever do.

But why is it so hard for some people?

HOMOPHOBIA / TRANSPHOBIA

Homophobia is described in *Merriam-Webster*'s dictionary as the "irrational fear of, aversion to, or discrimination against homosexuality or homosexuals." Note the "irratio-nal" part. The definition is also true of transphobia.

Homophobia, broadly speaking, comes from two places—inside and out: Other people airing antigay senti-ments, but also individuals themselves believing that there's something wrong with being gay or bi. Again, the same is true of transphobia. Many trans people will have grown up in environments where they have been led to believe there is something "weird" about swapping gender.

What if you believe there's something wrong with being gay, bi, or trans *and* you happen to BE gay, bi, or trans? This is more common than you might think. For ease, let's call this SELF-LOATHING.

If a young person thinks there is something wrong with being LGBTQ+, they're hardly likely to sing their identity from a balcony, Evita style, while waving a rainbow flag, are they?

Clearly, the issue here is **why do they think being LGBTQ+ is wrong?** I can't imagine anyone is born homophobic (or transphobic), so it must come from exter-nal sources, which brings us neatly to homophobia.

EXPLICIT HOMOPHOBIA

Sadly, there are small-minded bigots everywhere. "It's a free country," they say. "I can say what I like." Well, actually, inciting hatred is a criminal offense so, no, you can't.

- Some homophobes hate gay people because they think it's a part of their faith—we'll deal with that in chapter 6.

A: straight

- Some homophobes think it's dirty or disgusting. *eye roll*
- Some homophobes think that gay people will crawl down their chimneys and somehow convert them, like GAY VAMPIRES.

See? Irrational. Also stubborn, ill informed, and ignorant.

Transphobic people will be similarly disgusted with trans people, whether they think it's an impossibility for one to change their gender or if, as with gay people, they see trans people as EVIL SEX SIRENS WHO WILL FOOL YOU WITH THEIR GENDER SECRET. Talk to a certain type of cisgender person about Thailand, and within seconds they'll say something disparaging about the third gender, I promise you. Jerry Springer was terrible for this too.

B: LGBTQ

If a young person has grown up with parents or carers who have tutted every time a gay couple pops up on TV, they have been sent an unequivocal message that people do not approve of LGBTQ+ people. It doesn't even have to be parents or carers. If a peer group at school has spent ten years saying, "HA! THAT PENCIL CASE IS TOTALLY GAY!" the same message is being spread: That pencil case is terrible, and so are you.

THIS is why we must never use "gay" as a derogatory term. EVER.

The language we use is incredibly powerful and oh-so-easy to internalize. I'd like you to do a little activity. You will need a pen or a pencil. On the previous pages are two (genderless) people.

Keeping inside the lines (we're not animals), write all the words (both kind and unkind) you know that describe **straight** people in Person A and **LGBTQ+** people in Person B.

All done? I'm willing to bet that there's a lot more writing on Person B. Perhaps you've written "straight," "cis," or "normal" on the Person A.

With the possible exception of "breeder," there aren't an awful lot of derogatory terms about straight people, because our society is run predominantly by them.

However, Person B, I'd imagine, is covered from head to toe in abusive, offensive, ill informed, and damaging slurs. Am I right? Pretty much any words other than "gay," "lesbian," "bi," "transgender," "queer," or "curious" are inappropriate. This is why I personally won't list them in this book—I don't want to add to that toxicity. The words change, but there will always be brutal words to cut minority groups down to size. We call this an "obliteration exercise." Poor Person B is quite literally obliterated by insults.

There is no person left at all.

This is what homophobia does to young people. However thick our skin is, I imagine even the toughest young LGBTQ+ person has thought, "Oh God, this isn't going to be easy." And it isn't. Ever. Although we may be pleased we've figured ourselves out AND we may have the most supportive parents or caretakers in the universe, we all KNOW we're coming out into a world that is littered with hatefulness.

BUT it's this adversity that makes LGBTQ+ people strong. It's why we call ourselves proud. If you can recognize how much hate there is in the world and still come out as LGBTQ+, you, my friend, are a fighter.

LGBTQ+ people are STRONG. Because we have to be.

INSTITUTIONAL HOMOPHOBIA/TRANSPHOBIA

This is a far more insidious type of homophobia. In fact, some people would say this isn't homophobia at all, but I think it's just as damaging.

I'd like you to Google "happy couple" and see if there are any images of unambiguously gay couples.

Hint: **You won't see any.**

We could have carried out similar tests at the movies, on TV, in literature, or at the theater. With the possible exception of androgynous models like Andreja Pejić, Athena Wilson, and Casey Legler, or actresses such as Laverne Cox, you're not going to see proper representation of trans people either.

Despite an AWFUL LOT of people in the world being LGBTQ+, we are practically invisible in the media, something I find BAFFLING given that white gay men are hugely OVER-represented in media production.

Heteronormative values are forced down our throats from birth. Cinderella gets together with a dude she met once and lied to; the Little Mermaid rejects her entire culture for a guy; one princess even goes for a spot of bestiality and makes out with a FROG—but there are NO LGBTQ+ role models for kids.

It gets a little better in TV, books, and films. With a few notable exceptions (*And Tango Makes Three*, *The Family Book*, *Julián is a Mermaid*), preschool and tween content is almost exclusively straight. What's more surprising is that content aimed at teens isn't entirely balanced. Some TV series bravely include LGBTQ+ characters (let's name *Glee* and *Love, Victor as* outstanding providers of LGBTQ+ characters), and some authors (ahem) do feature LGBTQ+ characters in their novels. However, the number of gay characters probably doesn't match the proportion of LGBTQ+ teens in the real world, and too often LGBTQ+ characters are suicidal runaways—hardly representative.

Outside of the media, let's talk about schools. In history, did you learn about Alan Turing? Harvey Milk? What about Billie Jean King?

What does this all mean? Why is this homophobia? Because every time you access a media outlet (including the Internet—I get straight singles ads on Facebook) or walk into school, you are being told

STRAIGHT = NORMAL
CISGENDER = NORMAL

So just because something isn't being openly hostile toward LGBTQ+ people, it doesn't mean it's not quietly whispering that you're weird. Well, of course, you're FINE. It's the system that's total slug poop.

BEARD (noun)

A pretty woman attached to the arm of a closeted gay man to convince the rest of the world he is a straight, manly man, hence "beard."

Often to be found attached to the arms of closeted gay Hollywood actors such as [NAMES REDACTED].

LAVENDER MARRIAGE (noun)

A fake marriage designed to make

husband, wife, or both appear heterosexual in the public eye.

Popular in Hollywood with the likes of [NAMES REDACTED], in seemingly happy marriages.

Representation matters: because so few out LGBTQ+ actors are given opportunities to portray LGBTQ+ characters in Hollywood, it means few LGBTQ+ performers have been able to achieve the same success and influence as their cis, straight counterparts.

PARANOIA

Some would argue that both homophobia and transphobia have roots in suspicion and paranoia.

The less we understand a group in society—the less we bother to learn—the more misconceptions and worries we have. For a long time, LGBTQ+ people were relatively secretive, thus adding to the suspicion.

There was another major turning point, historically, that contributed to fear and paranoia, particularly about gay men, and that was the AIDS epidemic in the 1980s.

Let's have a history lesson:

The precise origin of HIV (human immunodeficiency virus) and AIDS (acquired immune deficiency syndrome) isn't known, although we can probably assume that the HIV infection, which attacks the immune system, jumped from apes to humans in Africa in the early twentieth century. Somehow, an unknown carrier of the virus traveled to the United States in the late 1970s, and the epidemic—and later pandemic—took hold.

For a time, HIV/AIDS was called GRID (gay-related immune deficiency), and by the time the medical world figured out that the illness could affect anyone—gay or not—the damage was already done. HIV/AIDS had become a "gay disease."

The reputation rose out of large gay communities in New York and California, where gay and bi men, who previously had no pressing need to use condoms, spread the infection at an alarming rate. Thousands of men died before clinicians could properly understand the disease.

Carriers of HIV were infected for years before becoming ill, and they infected others before they even realized they were carrying the virus. As they traveled the world, AIDS became a truly global problem, affecting EVERYONE, but the reputation of its being a "gay thing" stuck.

Ask ANY gay person who grew up in the 1980s, and they will tell you about a terrifying TV advertisement that featured people being squashed by a giant AIDS gravestone. It caused national panic. The problem was that people didn't properly understand the disease. Some people thought that you could be infected by sharing mugs or toilet seats with carriers of the virus. You can't, obviously—the virus is transmitted mostly through blood and semen—but ignoramuses became very wary of gay people. This wasn't just about, "they might try to trick me into butt sex," anymore; it was more, "this person could kill me."

It has taken thirty years to better educate people about HIV/ AIDS, and there are now effective treatments, but the stigma remains. Many out and proud gay men (and in this case, it IS mostly gay or bi men, not lesbians) will happily come out as gay but not as HIV positive for fear of judgment.

So for many awful, small-minded people, fear of gay people and fear of HIV/AIDS are permanently linked. Even if you're a child of the nineties, your parents will vividly remember the AIDS crisis. It's knowing their parents may still worry about HIV/ AIDS that keeps a lot of young gay men, in particular, trapped at the back of the closet with old coats and some mothballs.

While LGB people are largely better understood in society, the transgender community is years behind. People on TV and in newspapers endlessly debate if trans people are "real"; whether transgender children have been "brainwashed"; if trans people are trying to invade "safe spaces."

This is sheer paranoia.

Famous trans people like Laverne Cox have raised

sufficient awareness for small-minded people to start panicking over myths and stereotypes. But there have always been trans people. It's nothing new. We can only hope that as society adjusts to the increase in transgender representation the fuss dies down, and trans people can just get on with their lives without having to defend their existence every five minutes.

HOMOPHOBIC/TRANSPHOBIC BULLYING

Bullying is systematic abuse—verbal, physical, or mental. Homophobia (as discussed) is the irrational fear of LGBTQ+ people. Put them together, and you have people being bullied for their sexuality. Transphobic bullying is aimed at people perceived to be transgender.

If we're being picky, someone screaming, "Yo, fag!" at you in a street isn't homophobic bullying; it's homophobic abuse. There's a key difference—bullying suggests a repeated campaign against an individual or group.

Let's start with **physical abuse or bullying**. Well, assault is always a crime, so the law is on your side. Laws regarding LGBTQ+ people vary from state to state. Twenty-one states outlaw discrimination based on sexual orientation, and eighteen states outlaw discrimination based on gender identity or expression. Hate crimes based on sexual orientation or gender identity are also punishable by federal law under the Matthew Shepard and James Byrd, Jr. Hate Crimes Prevention Act of 2009. The FBI now monitors and tracks such hate crimes.

What's more, the Criminal Justice Act (2003) means that homophobic/transphobic crimes are dealt with more seriously and perpetrators given longer jail sentences in the UK, Ireland, and Canada. Some police forces also have an LGBTQ+ liaison officer to help victims of crime. If you have been assaulted, you should call 911 or visit your local police station. If an assault happens in a school, it is still assault and you should call the police or get someone at your school to do so.

Third-party reporting—where you can get someone you know to report a crime—means you don't even have to identify yourself if you would rather keep your sexuality a secret.

BULLYING IN SCHOOL

> When I was in Year 9, I came out and told my friends and they were OK with it, and then I told my dad. I asked if there was any support at school because I was being bullied. People used to pick on me, and one time a load of guys in a corridor stood up against the wall and said,

"Cover your arses." I told the teachers I was getting bullied and I went to the student counselor. After I spoke to her, she did a presentation about homophobic bullying. She got me to speak to everyone about it, which was really difficult. After the assembly...most of the bullies stopped; only a few carried on. People still come up to me and say how I was so brave.

—N, 17, Burgess Hill, UK

HOW TO CHALLENGE HOMOPHOBIC LANGUAGE

"That's so gay" and "No homo" are still used way too often in schools. What can you do if you hear it? A QUIFF system:

- Question: What do you mean by that?
- Understanding: "Do you know what 'gay' actually means?"
- Institution: "This school is a tolerant place; you can't say that."
- Feel: "I consider that offensive and homophobic."
- Funny: "Oh, wow, you're right, those shoes DO love each other even though they're both female."

You should only challenge homophobic or transphobic language if it is safe to do so—don't get into fights or put yourself at risk.

Homophobic and transphobic bullying is still a huge problem in schools. Why? If you asked most young people, "Do you hate gay people?" they'd probably say no. I think it's because ALL bullying is a problem in schools, and in such close quarters, people will lash out in any way they can—so whether it's your hair, your weight, your glasses, your braces, your clothes, OR your perceived sexuality, people will always find something to make fun of.

THAT DOESN'T MAKE IT OKAY.

You can, of course, do your bit by not making fun of other people. I don't think anyone is blameless when it comes to high school bullying. I think, on any given day, an individual can be both a bully and a victim.

Note how I said PERCEIVED sexuality. Remember, it's not just LGBTQ+ people who experience homophobic bullying—plenty of straight people have homophobic slurs made against them too.

The impact of homophobic bullying is huge. Gay rights charity Stonewall conducted research and found that fifty percent of young LGBTQ+ students had skipped school because of it, while seventy percent said it had affected their achievement at school. Well, that's just not okay.

Homophobic and transphobic bullying can take many forms:

- Verbal abuse (name-calling)
- Rumor spreading
- Exclusion (being left out of stuff)
- Cyber bullying (online or text messages)

- Death threats
- Physical violence
- Sexual assault

The law is on your side again. BY LAW a school has to tackle all forms of bullying AND provide a safe space. Schools must also take POSITIVE steps to make young LGBTQ+ people feel included—it's not enough for schools to merely tolerate us.

Be a SQUEAKY WHEEL: If you politely make enough noise at school, someone will eventually oil the gears.

DOUGLAS'S STORY

In 2008, I moved back to Scotland after having lived abroad—a sixteen-year-old with my mind set on going to university in two years' time.

"Aye, see that new boy from Canada? F**kin' poof."

What Kyle had said to Graeme in the corridor, oblivious to my presence, stuck with me. *How did he know?* I thought. *Where has all this come from? I barely know him!*

Having spoken to me once previously, he had made all of the assumptions he needed to start a two-year campaign of fear and isolation in my final years at high school. I could put it down to his immaturity—he was a year younger than me—but that only washes so many times. There were outright verbal attacks and a few physical attacks in PE by Kyle and Graeme. Trying to explain why you've got massive bruises down your side from being hit repeatedly with hockey sticks isn't easy to do. Somehow, I managed to explain it away.

I must admit, I look back at what happened and scream at my naivety for not having said anything sooner. In my last class on a Friday, I was discussing with a friend whom I had told I was gay what our plans for the weekend were. The plans involved seeing my then boyfriend on Saturday for one thing or another.

"It's so nice," said Gemma, "that you've managed to find yourself a boyfriend."

To my shock and total terror, a girl who sat behind me exclaimed, "You're gay?! I would never have guessed!"

This would have been bearable, but there were two problems: first being that my entire French class now knew, and the second that Kyle sat directly behind her. The last fifteen minutes of the class dragged on, and I can't remember much apart from my overwhelming sense of guilt, shame, and excruciating lack of hubris; people were demonizing and defending me all at once. Kyle finally had his confirmation: Douglas is gay.

I remember leaving early to collect my instruments from the music department and scurrying to my locker. By the time the rest of my [classmates] were down at the lockers, everyone knew. Some people were supportive, but Kyle, Graeme, and their friends took great delight in tormenting me as I gathered my things together.

I didn't want to return to school on Monday. I was deliberately late so as not to have to deal with anyone. By this point, my guidance [counselor] had a log of incidents I had reported to her.

A few weeks later, I was standing at my local train station waiting for a taxi to take me home. (I didn't and still do not feel safe walking home at night on my own.) Kyle and Graeme walked past me and started shouting abuse at me in the street. I had learned to deal with it in school but not in the street. They left and I got in a taxi. When I was finally in my house and safe, I cried. Why me? How could they find this acceptable? As far as I could make out, it was my bedroom practices they were ridiculing, but somehow they'd cut to the very core of my identity.

HOW TO TACKLE HOMOPHOBIC/ TRANSPHOBIC BULLYING AT SCHOOL

These steps would work well for any kind of bullying:

- If you feel you're being victimized, start a journal. Not like, "Dear Diary, he's so dreamy..."—more like names, dates, times, and places. List reliable witnesses to the incident(s).

- This is the tough part. Tell someone you trust and show them your journal.

- I KNOW—if you tell someone, it'll only get worse, right? WRONG. Your silence is what people rely on to control you. Bullying is all about power and control. If you play along with what your aggressor wants, you are giving them all the power.

- Your journal (and witnesses) will be very hard to argue with. A lot of young people think they won't be believed. YOU WILL. If the first teacher is unresponsive, go over their head. Find someone who will listen. Again, you're in control.

- Teachers are also under scrutiny. NO teacher or school wants to be perceived as homophobic or transphobic—their job or reputation would be on the line. They WILL help you.

- If you have been physically or sexually assaulted, you should call the police.

- What will happen next? Well, it depends on the school and the circumstances. By law, they have to act. I'm not gonna lie—the situation probably won't go away, but if you persist, your school will have to take tougher and tougher action to provide a safe space for you.

My advice is NEVER TAKE IT. As hard as it is, FIGHT.

As a final word on bullying, be aware that the day you leave school, your life as a young LGBTQ+ person will improve, but only because everyone's life improves when they leave school. It's become the slogan of the anti-homophobic-bullying movement, but **IT GETS BETTER.**

DISCRIMINATION IN THE WORKPLACE

About a year in[to my MTF transition], six months after I started presenting as myself full-time, my employer, which had seemed understanding at first, took steps toward showing me the door. I wound up saving them the legal hassle and just quitting, because it was getting unbearable. There is essentially no protection, and you are definitely going to change jobs at some point, either because they fire you or because they make things very unpleasant until you leave voluntarily. As an example of unpleasantness, it's also fairly common (as happened to me) that they'll ask you to limit your bathroom usage

> to a single-occupancy facility if they have one; in my
> case, the only one available was an elevator ride away
> and badly ventilated, so it smelled horrible, unlike the
> normal facilities in that building. I also know several trans
> women who are required by their employers to use the
> men's room.
>
> —Irene, 33, New Jersey

But what if life doesn't improve once you head into the working world? As discussed, there are small-minded people everywhere, I'm afraid—in your office, your hospital, your police station, anywhere you can imagine. But more good news! Once again the law is on your side: Being LGBTQ+ is a "protected class" (which I like because it makes us sound like a beautiful, rare butterfly on the verge of extinction in Java or something). It means, legally, you cannot be discriminated against when applying for a job, in education, when buying or renting property, or when accessing public services (for example, doctors or dentists).

Once you have a job, you cannot be fired because you're LGBTQ+; get less pay than a straight, cisgender colleague; be held back for promotion; or be fired (because you're LGBTQ+). If you're just plain crap at your job, then you're on your own, obviously.

If you think you have been discriminated against in the workplace, you can speak to your human resources department (if you have one) or get mediation from an outside agency such as Lambda Legal (see the "Helpful Websites and Numbers and Stuff" section for contact details). You can also go to your local Lambda Legal office. These sorts of disputes are often settled in court.

NO LAUGHING MATTER

Earlier, I said that it wasn't all Kylie and canapés, and I wasn't kidding. Homophobia kills. The following statistics are REAL and are why we all have to stand up against hate.[*]

- 19–29 percent of gay and lesbian students and 18–28 percent of bisexual students experienced dating violence in the last year.
- 14–31 percent of gay and lesbian students and 17–32 percent of bisexual students had been forced to have sexual intercourse at some point in their lives.
- LGBTQ+ youth were more likely than heterosexual youth to report high levels of bullying and substance use.

---

[*] Except where stated, all statistics courtesy of the Center for Disease Control and Prevention, Youth Risk Behavior Surveys (2001–2009).

- Students who were questioning their sexual orientation reported more bullying, homophobic victimization, unexcused absences from school, drug use, feelings of depression, and suicidal behaviors than either heterosexual or LGB students.
- A nationally representative study of adolescents in grades 7–12 found that lesbian, gay, and bisexual youth were more than twice as likely to have attempted suicide as their heterosexual peers.
- More studies are needed to better understand the risks for suicide among transgender youth. However, one study interviewing 55 transgender youth found that about 25 percent reported suicide attempts.
- Lesbian, gay, bisexual, and questioning teens are at least twice as likely as their heterosexual peers to use illegal drugs (San Diego State University study, 2018).

BOOM!

That was a distressing bomb detonating in your face. Yeah, I know this all makes for hugely depressing reading, but I'm all about the TRUTH. Clearly, being LGBTQ+ does not automatically make you depressed or suicidal, but the fact is that young LGBTQ+ people, when exposed to hatred or homophobia or when living with anxiety and threat, are bound to be vulnerable to mental health problems.

This is why all of us—all LGBTQ+ people, young and old—are still working for greater acceptance and challenging homophobia. Even a book like this would have been unthinkable ten years ago. It's CRAY! A book about YOU in a school library! What next?!

Hopefully, as tolerance, understanding, and visibility of LGBTQ+ people increases, homophobia will die out with the ignorant people it lingers in.

CHAPTER 6
HATERZ GON' HATE

Aside from a bit of pesky self-loathing, there are more practical reasons why people might choose not to identify as lesbian, gay, bisexual, or trans—or at the very least keep it under their hat. Depending on where you live and the faith you're born into, circumstances can vary wildly. This section, although hardly filled with LOLs, I'm afraid, is really important because, although it's pretty mega being a gay, it's far from comfortable for thousands of people all around the world. And, who knows, **we** might be able to make a little difference.

What's annoying is that homophobia is a cultural thing. In ancient times, people were super open-minded about gay shiz. Look at Sappho on her island; check out the same-sex culture of the Greeks and Romans. I'm afraid the tide turned when Christian missionaries took it upon themselves to travel the world to tell everyone how marriage should be done. From there, it was downhill all the way as far as the acceptance of homosexuality was concerned.

If you are reading this book in the U.S., Canada, the UK, or pretty much anywhere in Europe, you should feel very lucky indeed because while bitchy haterz be throwing shade, at least you have the law on your side. As discussed, in the U.S., you are actively protected.

HISTORY LESSON

Although it seems unbelievable, it was only in 2003 that the Supreme Court finally invalidated so-called "Sodomy Laws" in the last fourteen states to have them. Before 1962, male homosexual behavior was illegal in all states and could be punished with imprisonment or hard labor.

The age of consent (the age at which you can consent to sexual intercourse) varies depending on your state. In a few states, young gay couples have a higher age of consent, which is a form of discrimination. Most states have thankfully now repealed such laws. Wherever you are in United States, it's worth knowing where you stand with the law—what are your rights? What can you do to improve LGBTQ+ rights in your area?

Basically, my friends, sometimes being LGBTQ+ in the U.S. is a bit crappy, but, as you're about to learn, it could be far, FAR worse...

AROUND THE WORLD IN (ALMOST) EIGHTY GAYS

We didn't choose where we were born. We just popped out where our parent happened to be nine months after we were conceived. Similarly, we didn't choose to be gay or bi—our same-sex attraction has been there for as long as we can remember. Likewise, trans people, more often than not, have always felt they weren't in the correct body or at least felt an unease with gender norms.

In an ideal world, it wouldn't matter where you were born OR what your sexual orientation is, but this total lottery is having a severe impact on people all over the world. The U.S. may have wised up some over the past fifty years, but other countries are comparatively in the dark ages concerning LGBTQ+ rights.

All aboard for what I call the TOUR OF SHAME—as of 2020, these are the countries and territories where human rights are more like human wrongs (see what I did there?).

COUNTRIES WHERE NEITHER MEN NOR WOMEN CAN HAVE SAME-SEX SEX

Afghanistan, Algeria, Angola, Antigua and Barbuda, Barbados, Botswana, Burundi, Cameroon, Chad, Comoros, Dominica, Eritrea, Ethiopia, Gambia, Guinea, Guyana, Iran, Liberia, Malawi, Malaysia, Maldives, Mauritania, Morocco, Nigeria, Oman, Qatar, Saint Lucia, Saint Vincent and the Grenadines, Saudi Arabia, Senegal, Solomon Islands, Somalia, South Sudan, Sri Lanka, Syria, Tanzania, Tunisia, Uganda, United Arab Emirates, Western Sahara, Yemen, Zambia and some parts of Nigeria and Zanzibar, which belongs to Tanzania

COUNTRIES WHERE TWO MEN CANNOT HAVE SEX BUT THERE ARE NO RULES REGARDING WOMEN

Bangladesh, Bhutan, Brunei, Cook Islands, Eswatini, Grenada, Guyana, Jamaica, Kenya, Kiribati, Kuwait, Lebanon, Mauritius, Myanmar, Namibia, Pakistan, Palestine-Gaza, Papua New Guinea, Saint Kitts and Nevis, Samoa, Sierra Leone, Singapore, Togo, Tonga, Tuvalu, Turkmenistan, Uzbekistan, Zimbabwe, and Chechen Republic in Russia

COUNTRIES THAT OFFICIALLY HAVE LEGAL RIGHTS FOR LGBTQ+ PEOPLE, BUT LGBTQ+ PEOPLE FACE PERSECUTION

Egypt, Indonesia, Iraq, Poland, Russia

COUNTRIES THAT APPLY THE DEATH PENALTY — YES DEATH — FOR SAME-SEX COUPLES

Afghanistan, Brunei, Gaza Strip, Iran, Libya, Mauritania, Pakistan, Qatar, Saudi Arabia, Somaliland, Sudan, UAE, Yemen, and some parts of Nigeria and Somalia, and the Chechen Republic in Russia

These tables are accurate as of early 2020. With any luck, the lists will shrink all the time until there's no need for this roll call of shame.

Countries DO change their stance; for example Mozambique recently decriminalized same-sex activity...

Woo-hoo! Cake for everyone. When this book was first published in 2014, same-sex activity in India was legal, then it was illegal, and now it's legal again! Hurrah!

However—and it's a big however—just because any remaining countries have legalized same-sex behavior doesn't mean that it's EASY to get your funky sex dance on without repercussions. In many places, Indonesia being a good example, it is legal to have same-sex sex, but people would face great hardship if they were out.

Furthermore, the vast majority of "legal" countries still have all kinds of hideously homophobic legislation in place—no same-sex marriage or civil partnership, no adoption laws...many fail to provide even the most basic protection beyond, "It's legal, what more do you want?" Clearly, this isn't good enough, and campaigners still have a long way to go.

It's easy to think of gay-illegal places as being far, far away. Too far away to worry about. Well, how about Russia, where LGBTQ+ groups are being persecuted despite their legal status? What about Greece, where gay men and female prostitutes are facing mandatory HIV testing against their will? Scary, scary stuff.

BRYAN'S STORY

> The situation in Singapore is very strange. Even though gay people are becoming more and more visible, we have no legal rights. We have Pink Dot SG, which is a bit like Pride and we have "Arts Venues" which are places for gay people to meet up. I have never known anybody to be arrested, but it is illegal for two men to have sex. I personally don't understand it. Singapore is a beautiful and tolerant place, so it's hard to understand why we don't have laws to protect us.
>
> —"Bryan," 21, Singapore.

TRANSGENDER—GLOBAL SITUATION

Most countries around the globe now have *some* laws in place regarding the legal recognition of transgender people, although those rights and, vitally, how they're enforced, varies wildly.

- Some countries offer full legal recognition for transgender people.
- Some countries (e.g., Thailand, Singapore, Japan) offer legal recognition only after an individual has had sex-reassignment surgery.

- Some countries (e.g., India, Bangladesh) recognize the 'third gender' but don't believe an individual has *changed* gender.
- In some countries (e.g., United States) your legal recognition varies according to where you live.

Just because a country has laws in place regarding LGBTQ+ people doesn't mean it's a "safe place" to live. In the first six months of 2020, at least twenty-eight trans people in the United States were murdered. Let that sink in for a minute. I did say this book wasn't always a LOLfest, didn't I?

WHAT CAN YOU DO TO HELP?

Personally, I don't think it's enough to be upset about the treatment of LGBTQ+ people across the world. We have to do our little bit, right? For one thing, in the box of gay-illegal countries, I've set in bold places which are popular vacation destinations.

Step One: Don't Go There

Seriously, hit countries where it hurts—tourist dollars. For one thing, you won't be able to date while you're there, and for another (and more seriously), what if you had to rely on the police or hospitals in a place where you aren't legally recognized as having equal rights?

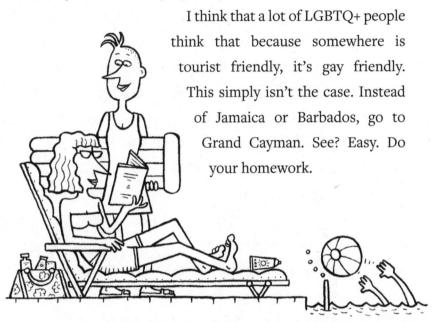

I think that a lot of LGBTQ+ people think that because somewhere is tourist friendly, it's gay friendly. This simply isn't the case. Instead of Jamaica or Barbados, go to Grand Cayman. See? Easy. Do your homework.

Step Two: Support Charity

We can help the fight by supporting groups doing the fighting for us.

Amnesty International: Challenges governments and authorities to fulfill their responsibility to protect LGBTQ+ people from such abuses. The organization campaigns to protect human rights defenders who put themselves at risk by speaking out against abuses based on sexuality or gender identity.

International Lesbian, Gay, Bisexual, Trans and Intersex Association (ILGA): ILGA's aim is to work for the equality of lesbian, gay, bisexual, trans, and intersex people and their liberation from all forms of discrimination. The group seeks to achieve this aim through the worldwide cooperation and mutual support of their members.

Gay & Lesbian Alliance Against Defamation (GLAAD): A media pressure group who ensure fair and diverse representation of the LGBTQ+ community in print, TV, and film in the U.S.

The Kaleidoscope Trust: Urges the British government, the Commonwealth, the European Union, and others to use their power and influence to support the rights of LGBTQ+ people. The trust works with parliamentarians, government ministers, officials, and policy makers to try to effect real change in the lives of LGBTQ+ communities around the world.

The Trevor Project: Founded in 1998 by the creators of the Academy Award–winning short film *Trevor*, the Trevor Project is the leading national organization providing crisis intervention and suicide prevention services to lesbian, gay, bisexual, transgender, queer, and questioning young people under twenty-five years of age.

The Attic Youth Center: The Attic Youth Center creates opportunities for LGBTQ+ youth to develop into healthy, independent, civic-minded adults within a safe and supportive community, and promotes the acceptance of LGBTQ+ youth in society. From what was once a weekly support group, The Attic has grown into a nationally recognized, multi-service youth organization, and is now one of the largest community centers in the U.S. committed exclusively to serving LGBTQ+ youth and allies.

Stonewall Community Foundation: Stonewall is renowned for its campaigning and lobbying. Some major successes include helping achieve the equalization of the age of consent, lifting the ban on lesbians and gay men serving in the military, securing legislation allowing same-sex couples to adopt, and the repeal of Section 28 (which prevented same-sex education in schools). More recently, Stonewall has helped secure civil partnerships and ensured that the Equality Act (2010) protected lesbians and gay men in terms of goods and services (for example, hotels can't refuse you and your partner a room because you're a same-sex couple).

Since 2014, Stonewall also protects the rights of trans and nonbinary people too.

All of these groups rely on donations. This means you need to jolly well stick your hand in your pocket and donate whatever you can. Some charities are listed in the "Helpful Numbers and Websites and Stuff" section at the back of this book.

THE QUEERS VERSUS RELIGION

You know when we said it's not very nice when people say that ALL gay men are like this or ALL lesbians are like that? WELL, it's similarly bogus to claim that ALL Christians think like this or ALL Muslims think like that. Before we get into a discussion about what each of the main religions thinks about homosexuality, it's important to state that all people of faith are individuals, more than capable of forming their own opinions away from scripture.

To be honest, most people of faith probably don't give a flying fig about who you're kissing—they're probably worrying about their gas bill or whether they left their hair straighteners on.

However, although most religious people are somewhat progressive, there are individuals and regimes that insist on clinging to multi-thousand-year-old bits of paper in the name of hate. If you look back at the list of gay-illegal countries, they tend to be the ones where the legal system is tied to a religious regime—not naming names but, like, you know, Saudi Arabia.

Before I tear some old religious stuff to shreds, **I have** faith that the vast, vast majority of religious people use (whichever) God's teaching to find tolerance and love for all mankind. And also womankind (yeah, some religions are mega sexist too).

Most people of religion see their sacred texts as a general guide for life—moral guidance, as it were. The problem comes when a minority take the written words literally—and the meaning of some of these words may even have been misinterpreted. Sacred stories and poems were written down by humans hundreds of years ago and so may have errors or mistranslations or additions. It's sort of like playing a game of telephone that's lasted for centuries— some things are bound to get lost along the way.

The closest thing I personally have to a prophet is Madonna. Now what if I went around taking everything she said literally? Look at the lyrics to "Express Yourself" and "Material Girl"... contradictory at best, I'm sure you'll agree!

Let's take a look at the main world religions and examine their traditional views first on homosexuality, then transgenderism.

1. Hinduism and Buddhism

Let's start with the positive. Hinduism and Buddhism are way chilled out about both homosexuality and trans issues. Hindu art depicts various figures engaging in same-sex acts, while the whole point of Buddhism is about being at one with the world, which, in this case, includes us.

Hurrah for Hinduism and Buddhism!

2. Christianity

As you know, there are various branches of the Christian church, and they each take a different stance on homosexuality. Here's a best-fit guide:

- **Catholic Church:** Homosexuality is considered a sin.
- **Methodist Church:** Pretty cool comparatively.
- **Anglican Church:** Progressive but resistant. Same-sex marriage is OK for normal folks but not priests.
- **Quakers:** Mad cool. They've been cool for years.
- **Baptists:** They have a huge problem with the gays, I'm afraid.

So what's the big problem? Well, it's all about TRANSLATION and LANGUAGE. There are lots of translations of the Bible (the Christian holy book), and all of them are slightly different. The odd word here and there looks pretty bad for homosexuality.

The issues stem from two key parts of the Bible. The quotes below are from the American Standard Version, and I've put them in a SCARY FONT. No reason...

"AND THEY CALLED UNTO LOT, AND SAID UNTO HIM, WHERE ARE THE MEN THAT CAME IN TO THEE THIS NIGHT? BRING THEM OUT UNTO US, THAT WE MAY KNOW[*] THEM." —Genesis 19:5

"EVEN AS SODOM AND GOMORRAH, AND THE CITIES ABOUT THEM, HAVING IN LIKE MANNER WITH THESE GIVEN THEMSELVES OVER TO FORNICATION AND GONE AFTER STRANGE FLESH,[†] ARE SET FORTH AS AN EXAMPLE, SUFFERING THE PUNISHMENT OF ETERNAL FIRE." —Jude 1:7

So what's goin' on here? In a nutshell, the towns of Sodom and Gomorrah used to be in the Jordan Valley until divine judgment was passed and they were destroyed by heavenly fire. Sounds like an awesome episode of *Buffy* until you realize that people use this story to persecute people.

In some interpretations of the Hebrew text (versions

---

* (In this instance, "to know" is thought to mean "to know intimately.")

† ("Strange flesh" is thought to mean, in this case, "sex.")

of this story appear in the Torah, Bible, and Quran), it's thought the behavior that displeased God so much was homosexuality.

This is WIDELY open to interpretation as we shall soon discover. More eye-roll inducing admonition from the book of Leviticus:

"THOU SHALT NOT LIE WITH MANKIND, AS WITH WOMAN-KIND: IT IS ABOMINATION." —Leviticus 18:22

"AND IF A MAN LIE WITH MANKIND, AS WITH WOMANKIND, BOTH OF THEM HAVE COMMITTED ABOMINATION: THEY SHALL SURELY BE PUT TO DEATH; THEIR BLOOD SHALL BE UPON THEM." —Leviticus 20:13

Way harsh.

How to Argue with Christians

So if you have the misfortune to stumble onto a literalist, homophobic Christian, how do you go about defending yourself? Knowledge is power, my friend.

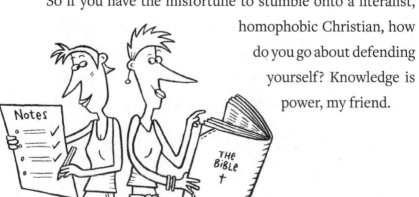

IF THEY COME AT YOU WITH "IT'S IN THE BIBLE!"

Let's talk about translation. The Bible has been translated and interpreted many, many times. We can't be one hundred percent certain what the original even said, so it's insane to take it literally. This is true of any translated or interpreted text. Even the various modern versions of the Bible are different, so how can one possibly take it all literally?

Point out that the text was written thousands of years ago. Times have changed. The messages are still somewhat applicable, but we have to adapt them for modern living. Also point out that ALL of the above extracts are out of context, and at the end of the day, they are stories, not laws (even the Apostle Paul decreed this).

Contexts change. The Bible repeatedly refers to going after taxmen—who at the time were crooked. You don't hear about Christians chasing after the IRS with flaming torches, do you?

Also, lady lovers, as the problem all stems from "sodomy," lesbians are automatically off the hook anyway! Whoop!

Finally, in the New Testament, based on the teachings of Jesus, Jesus said precisely NOTHING on the subject. As we know, Jesus taught nothing but love and tolerance.

Personally, I think Jesus, had he lived today, would be at every Pride march.

Here's a Twist You Might Not Have Seen Coming

There's some fairly convincing evidence of gay love IN THE BIBLE almost three thousand years prior to *Queer as Folk*. That's right. In the book of Second Samuel, besties David and Jonathan may have been a little more than friends! Check it out:

> "I AM DISTRESSED FOR THEE, MY BROTHER JONATHAN: VERY PLEASANT HAST THOU BEEN UNTO ME: THY LOVE TO ME WAS WONDERFUL, PASSING THE LOVE OF WOMEN." 2 Samuel 1:26 (You go, gurlz!)

And the gals were getting on board the sexy Bible love train too. The story of Ruth and Naomi reads like an episode of *Desperate Housewives* on crack—there's a LOT of husband swapping—but some scholars read their journey as same-sex love.

Finally, there are various bits of the Bible that are conveniently missing—see the Gospel of Mary—so, as ever, we mustn't wholly trust such ancient sources of information.

3. Islam

A little like the Bible, there's not an awful lot in the Quran to explicitly forbid homosexual behavior, although it also refers to the people of Sodom and Gomorrah, this time with a more explicit focus on rape, not homosexuality. Well, we already know how to respond to that story, don't we?

HOW TO ARGUE WITH SODOM AND GOMORRAH

Firstly, the phrase "to know" (from the Hebrew) very rarely means "to have sex." In this case, it most likely means "interrogate." Secondly, it is thought the "strange flesh" refers to that of the angels or possibly bestiality. In either case, most Biblical scholars agree that the towns were struck down primarily for their greed and uncharitable nature. There is no CLEAR reference to homosexuality.

HOW TO ARGUE WITH LEVITICUS

OK, I grant you this one is a little more clear cut, BUT—there's a big BUT (tee-hee). Basically, Leviticus is meant to be a list of instructions from Moses to the Levites and, yes, the one above was one of the rules. But, luckily for us, the rest of the list was CRAY. So anyone throwing a bit of Leviticus your way should also be prepared to:

Sell their daughter into slavery.

Never make any physical contact with a woman on her period. Burn bulls.

Never eat shellfish (also an abomination, so BEWARE THE PRAWN). Never trim the hair around their head. This is forbidden.

So, as you can see, you'd have to be a pretty massive hypocrite to use this one as an argument against homosexuality.

The larger problem comes from the Hadith, or teachings of Muhammad. These are...erm...less ambiguous.

"WHOEVER YOU FIND COMMITTING THE SIN OF THE PEOPLE OF LUT (LOT), KILL THEM, BOTH THE ONE WHO DOES IT AND THE ONE TO WHOM IT IS DONE." —Sunan al-Tirmidhi

Well, at least it doesn't discriminate between the bottom and top.

How to Argue with Muslims

The good news is that the Quran is on your side. NOWHERE in there does Allah state a punishment for homosexual behavior. What's more, the Quran actively encourages diversity, as Allah created that too:

"O MANKIND! WE CREATED YOU FROM A SINGLE (PAIR) OF A MALE AND A FEMALE AND MADE YOU INTO NATIONS AND TRIBES THAT YE MAY KNOW EACH OTHER (NOT THAT YE MAY DESPISE EACH OTHER). VERILY THE MOST HONORED OF YOU IN THE SIGHT OF ALLAH IS (HE WHO IS) THE MOST RIGHTEOUS OF YOU. AND ALLAH HAS FULL KNOWLEDGE AND IS WELL ACQUAINTED (WITH ALL THINGS)." —Yusuf Ali Quran 49:13

Regarding the Hadith, as with Leviticus, there are various rules that very few people would follow today—seduction by women is on a par with homosexual acts, so, it would seem, is drinking wine. I'm sure we wouldn't kill people for these things.

Moreover, the sharia law sets no specific punishment for homosexual behavior—recommending the death penalty only be used for adultery, renouncing the faith and murder. Most Muslim countries don't enforce these punishments (side eye at those who do).

4. Judaism

Not being funny, but these guys kinda started it. The parts of the Bible that deal with homosexuality came from the bits based on the Torah (the Pentateuch), so it's pretty much the same story—the general negative feeling toward homosexuality comes from Sodom and Gomorrah and Leviticus, in this case called Vayiqra.

As with Christianity, there are many branches of the Jewish faith and, unsurprisingly, the Orthodox branch tends to be the most, well, orthodox. One of the most popular forms of Judaism, **Reform Judaism**, is way more chilled and doesn't prohibit gay, lesbian, or bisexual couples from entering the faith. So let's all send them a cookie.

LUKE'S STORY

Apparently as a boy of around four or five years old, there was an occasion in which I came home in tears from school—someone had told me that God didn't exist.

As a child I was also known for my reenactments of Disney films and performing Cher's "The Shoop Shoop Song" for anyone that would sit around long enough to endure it; this led my parents to believe that I'd either be a vicar or an actor (why actor and not drag queen I'm not sure; I'm told I played the part of Cinderella wonderfully). It turns out that I'm neither a vicar nor actor (nor drag queen, although I do have the legs for it) but I still retain that same faith I had twenty-odd years ago.

I grew up not in a traditionally Christian family, but we began to attend church when we moved to Sussex shortly before my ninth birthday and it soon became a very important part of my life and my development.

Much of my free time as a teenager was spent volunteering with the children's and youth [groups] at our local Baptist church, and I had a close group of friends who [did] the same. The painful irony was that they only knew just one aspect of me, no matter how much time we spent in each other's company.

Growing up and from a young age knowing that

you're gay (I asked out my first "boyfriend" at age ten) yet being reminded fairly consistently that "God's best is man and woman" is a damaging place to be. It causes many people to lose their faith, many to self-harm, and many to take their lives. It's a hurtful place that countless young people and adults alike still find themselves in today and the Church has a lot of work to do to make amends there.

However, this being said, I consider myself to be in an incredibly privileged position now that I've come through those imposed dark places. I came to own my faith personally and not have it prescribed to me by dogmatic teaching; my theological studies aided this journey and allowed me to realize I belong to two beautiful, charismatic, joyful, and alive communities that in spite of their differences, often look at life in just the same way.

Being a Christian who also happens to be gay, or being a gay man who also happens to have a faith, is often a troublesome path to tread, neither community really quite understanding how you can belong to both fully, but I find it to be an incredibly energizing adventure to be part of.

As a Christian I believe that God is love and where there is love God is there; one of the most loving communities I know belongs to "the gays" and so this is where I know God dwells.

RELIGION AND TRANSGENDERISM

This one throws up more problems. Before we start, it's worth noting that gender reassignment, as we know it today, wasn't possible when the key holy texts were being written. Therefore there really isn't a precedent for it. There are, however, a few passages on cross-dressing which have been skewed to encapsulate all gender dysphoria.

Paradoxically, Islam takes a fairly chilled view on this. There's nothing specific in the Quran, and the Hadith takes issue only where "cross-dressing" is used for sex work. However, in some countries, gender reassignment surgery (often male to female) is seen as a "cure" for homosexuality, which is a crime. This clearly isn't ideal.

Christianity and Judaism have more defined and, indeed, negative views about gender reassignment. In Deuteronomy of the Old Testament (and similarly in the Torah), there appears the following passage:

"A WOMAN SHALL NOT WEAR THAT WHICH PERTAINETH UNTO A MAN, NEITHER SHALL A MAN PUT ON A WOMAN'S GARMENT; FOR WHOSOEVER DOETH THESE THINGS IS AN ABOMINATION UNTO JEHOVAH THY GOD."
—Deuteronomy 22:5

There are also references to eunuchs (men with their sexual organs removed) not being able to enter the temple.

As with the passages that address homosexuality, trans people are more than able to defend themselves should the Bible or Jewish Scripture be used to attack them. In the case of Deuteronomy, the text appears to refer to cross-dressing, not gender dysmorphia and, given the era it was written in, could actually be about practices of pagan fertility cults at the time.

Furthermore, the eunuchs back then weren't castrated to change gender; many were slaves who had their bits chopped off against their will. Once more we can see that many of the rules applicable to the people of biblical times simply aren't relevant anymore.

Finally, in the book of John, the author talks about Jesus's inclusive view of those born with birth defects, and I think we can argue being born the wrong gender is indeed one such defect. I love it when you can actually use the Bible to argue in our favor.

Furthermore, the concept of third gender stems from Hindu teaching and philosophy. This category encompasses all genders that exist outside of simply male and female and is often legally recognized. In some cultures and rituals, members of the third gender are revered as having almost magical powers and are considered lucky. So, see, it's not all bad, is it?

A FINAL NOTE

A dear friend once told me, "YOU CAN'T ARGUE WITH CRAZY." Someone else once said, "HATERZ GON' HATE." Put these two pieces of wisdom together and you kind of have the situation we're in. People using religion to hate LGBTQ+ people are going to do so however well we argue our case. You'll spout logic until you're blue in the face and some homophobes will continue to hate.

I believe if you wanted to piece together a convincing argument about why steak and kidney pie was sinful, you would be able to use religious texts to help your campaign— they are old enough and vague enough to damn almost anything.

All we can do is rest assured that we are far from an abomination. Whether you believe in God as a creator or not, we were all born out of something very natural. We are one hundred percent organic. Like orange juice with pulp.

CHAPTER 7
COMING OUT

Resisting reruns of *SpongeBob SquarePants* while revising; avoiding the sharklike gaze of your cruel, capricious math teacher; trying to think of something hilarious but alluring to say to that person you're dying to kiss—your school years are pretty tough. As if all that wasn't hard enough, the average age at which people usually "come out" as gay, lesbian, or bi is now seventeen years old—while still in high school or college. Just one more thing to worry about, and it's not on the curriculum.

How to do it? When to do it? Whom do you tell? Do you tell anyone at all? Coming out is a potential minefield. One wrong step and your metaphorical gay leg will be blown clean off.

Seriously, though. For a young LGBTQ+ person, there is NOTHING more terrifying than the idea of telling your nearest and dearest that you are into people with the same genitalia as you or that you've pretty much had enough of your original gender. This fear is perfectly reasonable, but there are ways in which we can make the transition from "closet case" to "out and proud" as smooth as caramel.

WHAT IS "COMING OUT"?

In the olden days (and to this very day in some rather traditional quarters), fancy young society women, known as debutantes, were dressed up and paraded around for potential suitors and the like. These events were known as "coming out parties," and this is where we get the term "coming out." Before the First World War, the phrase meant more to come out into society.

These days, we refer in particular to "coming out of the closet," an American slang term for no longer concealing one's identity. Once you're ready to let the world know about your identity, you are no longer "closeted" or "on the down low."

The word identity is key. Coming out isn't when you first swap love juice with someone of your own gender, but rather the public adoption of a label. It's telling people.

As I've said numerous times, labels aren't for everyone. Lots of people may choose to have sexyfuntimes with people of the same gender without identifying as gay or lesbian, just as a gay man who has sex with a woman isn't automatically straight. ("Hallelu! He's seen the light!" Yeah, that's not gonna happen). The process of establishing an identity can take years. The good news is, no one is stuck with one label for their whole life.

Many people change their sexual identity as they become more comfortable with themselves and their sex lives.

The same is true of gender labels. Gender doesn't have to be concrete.

One only has to look at the thriving queer club scene to see hot young things experimenting with traditional gender roles. These have nothing to do with sexuality, as we've discussed.

At its core, coming out is the part where you tell someone what your sexual or gender orientation is—and that can be anything.

WHY COME OUT AT ALL?

Perhaps the real question is: Is there any benefit to coming out? The answer is almost certainly...

YES!

People cheerfully profess their religion, marital status, ethnic origin, and favorite food, but discussion of sexual orientation or gender remains uniquely taboo. Perhaps with good reason.

As we have learned, there are eighty countries where men and women can be prosecuted for having sex with someone of the same gender. MEGA POLITICAL SAD FACE.

If it is safe to come out, however, there are many benefits to doing so. At the end of the day, desires, crushes, dating, and relationships are a massive part of anyone's life, and hiding something so vital from your friends and family is both hard work and isolating. It may sound trite, but being yourself is good for you. Sharing is caring, yo!

> Coming out made me so much more confident—there isn't this part of me I'm pushing down around my friends and family. There are a host of things that go along with that ([being] able to dress myself how I want, hold my girlfriend's hand on the subway, voice my opinion on legislative issues related to LGBT rights, etc.), but ultimately, coming out has let me be myself, and that is a really amazing feeling.
>
> —Megan, 19, Boston

The single phrase mentioned time after time after time in the survey was **"a weight off my shoulders."** So cliché but so, so true.

On a more practical level, once a young person has come out as gay, lesbian, bisexual, or trans, it is that much easier to find like-minded people. There will be MILLIONS of LGBTQ+ youth groups across the U.S. The Human Rights Campaign is a great resource to find out what's available in your area.

Furthermore, once a person chooses to identify as gay, lesbian, bisexual, or trans, you'd be surprised by how supportive family and friends can be. Very often, parents and friends have already figured it out, and coming out leads to a closer, more honest relationship with the people you love the most. Perhaps best of all, they'll stop trying to fix you up with people who are the wrong sex!

Finally, don't underestimate the personal satisfaction and pride you'll feel at simply being yourself. It's freeing.

> There are so many [advantages to coming out] that it's hard to know where to start. The main things are to know that you will still be loved, and that you are happy and content in who you really are. I was so worried about how my family would react to my sexuality that it used to keep me awake at night...now I know how well [coming out to them] went, I wish that I had talked to them sooner. It took a few months to adjust to being open about my sexuality, but it definitely made me closer to my family. I did run into some issues with bullying

at school, being the first boy to "come out." Once I was accepted (begrudgingly) as a part of the school, I think it was easier for others to be honest. I was very lucky in that I had some good teachers, lots of friends, and my family for support.

—Mike, UK

WHY "STAY IN"?

Of course, there may be good reasons why people choose not to discuss their sexual or gender identity. For one, it does often seem that there are three choices—straight, gay, or bi. Sometimes it's just not that simple, so defining yourself may take more time.

Moreover, some communities and religions believe that homosexuality is wrong. That doesn't prevent anyone from being lesbian, gay, or bisexual but rather restricts their ability to be out, as this may mean they feel their parents and friends might not be supportive of them.

The worry of what family and friends might think or do is what keeps people in the closet more than any other factor, regardless of background. Remember, every out gay or bisexual man or woman and every out trans person has gone through this process and survived the ordeal. Most retain the family and friends they had before they came out.

WHEN IT GOES WRONG

The fear that you'll be disowned, shamed, and tossed out onto the street is absolutely the worst-case scenario and one that very rarely happens. There may be friends who are unable to accept your new identity, and that's sad, but you can always make new friends. The worst fear is that your family, especially your parents, might react badly. At first many do—I won't lie—but with time, nearly all build a bridge and get over it.

If (and I can't stress enough how rare this is) the situation becomes so bad that you have to leave home, there is support out there. Some people live with other family members or family friends. There's a list of groups near you at the back of the book.

> It started when my mom saw me hugging a friend on Facebook. She is Catholic—very Catholic—and for months I was getting, "You're gay—I'm gonna kick you out." After about two months of this, something in my head snapped and I said, "I'm not gay, I don't know what I am!" I was fourteen. Two days later I got kicked out. I had to work...I worked in a Chinese takeout [restaurant]. Eventually I became a chef, and now I own my home.
> —Shane, 23, Shoreham-By-Sea, UK

"I'm coming out. I want the world to know."

So you've decided you might identify as LGBTQ+? The hardest part—admitting it to yourself—is done. But how to tell everyone else?

The first time I came out was about six months after my Dean Cain–based revelation. I told a very close friend whom I trusted not to shout it from the rooftops. She had also done a very good job of signaling to me that she was A-OK with THE GAYS. As a young questioning person, you would do well to surround yourself with cool, open-minded people—it lubes the passage out of the closet, as it were.

I chose to tell her—well, "chose" isn't the right word; rather it popped out as I carried a treacle tart home from school one day. (I stress I had made the tart earlier in a home economics class. I don't just carry cakes around to make people like me.)

Predictably, my friend was cool and reassuring and herself came out as queer in the same conversation, so I felt a million times better. To this day, though, I cannot eat treacle tart without feeling like my world might come crashing in around me, as it did that night after I had come out—because even though my afternoon had been perfectly pleasant, the cat was now out of the bag, and I couldn't get the furry bugger back in it. That is always going to be scary.

I adjusted quickly. Over the following weeks, I talked about boys CONSTANTLY, making up for lost time, and within a few weeks I was happily telling my friend and a couple of other friends which boy I'd most like to kiss on the rugby team. It was all fine and I haven't looked back.

I came out to my parents much later—I waited until I was living away from home and able to support myself financially. You can decide if that was cowardly or sensible. In the end, my mom actually asked me outright and I answered her honestly. I got my stepmom to tell my dad!

The SECOND time I came out—this time as transgender—was just as stressful even though I was an adult. Once again, my parents were wonderful after a brief "the sky is falling" period.

Since this book originally came out in 2014, I've had thousands of emails from young people concerned about coming out, and I tell them the same thing: you will need PATIENCE. I had twenty-odd years and a year of therapy to prepare me for my transition...my parents had neither of those benefits. You have to give people time and space to adjust their mindset of you.

Every LGBTQ+ person's experiences are different, but here are the dos and don'ts of coming out:

Do	Don't
Tell someone you trust, someone you feel comfortable talking with, and who you think won't tell the whole world until you're ready.	Leave your Internet browser full of, erm, films of a certain persuasion. You'd be shocked how many people are outed this way.
Put feelers out as to your family's or friends' attitudes to LGBTQ+ people before discussing it with them. Listen to what they're saying about other gay people to get an idea of whether they're a "safe" person to tell.	Forget the professionals—teachers and doctors are trained to listen to exactly these sorts of issues, and they may offer valuable advice. You might even get a jazzy pamphlet.
Talk to people who've been through it all before—other LGBTQ+ people. See how they survived!	Be dramatic. Your sister's wedding is NOT the best time to leap into the aisle, block the bride's path, and scream: "I LOVE COCK."
Pick your moment—find a quiet, safe space.	Do it by email or text—the written word is easy to misinterpret. ("You're coming out where, honey? Will you still be home in time for dinner?" etc.)
Celebrate. Once you've done it, it can feel like you've opened Pandora's box, but the hardest part is done.	Come out because someone else, even a partner, says you should. You have to do it when YOU'RE ready.
Read this book!	Come out just because you have a boyfriend or girlfriend—those you tell are much more likely to think it's a "phase" that will last as long as the relationship.

DON'T JUST TAKE IT FROM ME

Every out gay or bisexual or trans man or woman has been through it all before!

> I first told my sister. We were talking in her bedroom when sexuality came up. I admitted to her that I didn't feel I was in the "normal" group but also didn't identify completely as LGBT. I explained to her the difference between sexual and romantic love. I told her that I could be romantically attracted to nearly everyone but wasn't sexually attracted to anyone.
>
> —Ali, 17, Arizona

> I waited a long time for someone to ask me my sexual orientation. I was ready for years, but decided I wouldn't tell anyone unless they asked because I felt no need to make something so private about myself a topic of conversation. Eventually I told a friend, but only because she had a crush on me and I didn't want to lead her on.
>
> —Josh, 24, Philadelphia

> I told my friend in the tiny music practice room in our school. It amuses me today to think that most people come OUT of the closet. I came out IN a closet. I thought I was bisexual at first, although, in retrospect, I think

that I was having difficulty understanding the difference between the strong kinship I felt with my female friends and the sexual attraction I had to other boys. It felt like a large part of puberty was finding out the answer to this conundrum.

—Rick, 29, UK

[I came out on a] residential trip to France. My gay friend asked me how I felt about her being gay, and I said I was OK. She asked me if I was straight. I said no. We carried on talking about how sh*t the French weather was when you had to do an assault course in the mud.

—Nina, 16, UK

[I first told] people at my halls of residence at uni. We went on a night out just before Christmas, and I made sure they were all there and told them one by one. The first was someone I had gotten really close to, and after that, admittedly with a drink or two inside me, it got easier.

—Chris, Manchester, UK

I first told a girl I was friends with at school. I was sixteen and we were at a party, and we went for a long walk and had a deep and meaningful [conversation]. She told me she was in love with another one of our friends, and I said I really fancied our art teacher.

—L, 28, Brighton, UK

Of course...it's not always so smooth. Coming out can be tough.

I told my girlfriend at the time, whom I'd been with for three years, about my thoughts and feelings regarding my desire to transition to female, my self-view as female, and my experimentation over the past number of years. She broke up with me then and there, refusing to discuss it.

—Laura, 21, UK

The first person I told was a female friend who believed she was in love with me. She was married and had made it clear that she was prepared to abandon that to be with me. I felt like I owed it to her to explain why that could never happen.

—BFL, 43, Minnesota

My stepmom discovered photos from the Internet that I had printed at college... It kind of went from there!

—Dani, 29, Newcastle upon Tyne, UK

A HANDY SCRIPT

Friends are relatively easy to come out to, as you've (presumably) picked mates who aren't total douches. Some LGBTQ+ people are in heterosexual or cisgender relationships when they figure it out, and it can be very hard to tell a partner that you're not (exclusively) sexually interested in them.

But most LGBTQ+ people worry the most about telling their parents. It really scares the plop out of us. Why? Well, they knew us as babies, and coming out (as gay, bi, or lesbian) is essentially offering a delightful insight into your sexual desires.

Something NO ONE enjoys saying: "Hey, Mom, you'll never guess what I like having up my bum!" See my point?

For trans people, some parents see it as a bit of a slap in the face. Like they GAVE you your assigned gender and they RAISED you accordingly. As with sexuality though, it often comes as no surprise, and many parents can be hugely supportive of transgender children—even very young ones. There are support groups, such as The Trevor Project and Trans Youth Equality Foundation, for parents of trans children (see "Helpful Numbers and Websites and Stuff" at the back of the book).

Coming out is as personal as your identity. The following is only a guide—a one-size-fits-all approach for you to adapt.

Pick Your Time

It might be spontaneous, or you might plan a specific time (although the build-up would be TORTURE). A lot of LGBTQ+ people seem to use the TV as a prompt; i.e., bringing it up when gay rights are mentioned in the news or when gay couples are shown in shows, which is pretty much every day. Whatever time you pick, I think a one-on-one conversation is always best.

Pick a Venue

Remember, your loved ones might need a bit of time to process, so I wouldn't recommend a mall changing room. Nine times out of ten, home is best, or at the very least an establishment that serves tea. Tea makes everything OK—remember that. (Do you have somewhere to go if they need some space—could you pop over to a friend's house?)

Is It Safe?

Your safety is more important than anything else on earth. Do you live in Saudi Arabia or one of the eighty-ish countries (see chapter 6) where you might be locked up or stoned to death? Look into getting a passport.

Joking aside, if your parents have expressed homophobic sentiments in the past, it may be wise to make a plan B should they react badly. A lot of people choose to wait until they have a degree of independence before taking this step. Make contact with gay youth groups—a list of which are at the back of this book—and ensure you have support should things go awry.

OK, so now we've set it all up, here are some openers:

"I really wanted to talk to you about something..."

Now, at this stage, it's possible your parent(s) might say, "Is this about your being gay?" VERY OFTEN parents have got an inkling. This is exactly how my mom dragged me out of the closet.

If they don't, however...

"For a while now, I've been attracted to men/women/ men AND women" or "I identify much more as a guy than I do a girl" (or vice versa).

Then...

"Nothing's changed. I'm still exactly the same person you know, and I hated keeping that a secret from you."

And then give them a chance to reply. You might be surprised and delighted.

> I told my parents I was bisexual at twenty. They were conservatively religious, but they told me they loved me just the same. I told them I was actually gay shortly after turning twenty-two, and this time they didn't bat an eyelid.
> —Stephen, 22, Johannesburg, South Africa

I told them both, although separately, as they are divorced, and each one was in a pub while we were having dinner. They were a little taken aback, but after a while, I think after they had thought about it for a bit, they realized that it explained a lot of my previous behavior and appearance. They couldn't care less now and are happy that I am happy.

—Jools, 38, Madrid, Spain

But what if they're not happy? Some likely objections:

Likely Objection	Response
Are you sure?	I really am. I've felt this way for a very long time. It's just that now I'm comfortable talking about it with you.
Is it a phase?	No. (See above.)
You're not gay*! (*or lesbian, bi, trans, etc.)	I am. I know this must be a bit of a shock, but I've always been this way. It just took me this long to figure it out.
Could you try not being...?	No. I've given this a lot of thought. I'm telling you because I need to be honest about who I am.
I don't believe it!	I've had loads of time to think about this. I understand you'll need some time to process what I'm telling you.

Don't tell anyone else!	I can't promise that. I can give you some time to think about what I've said, but I need to be honest about who I am.

Keep strong and listen to Lady Gaga's "Born This Way." Or simply present them with this very book and get them to turn to this chapter!

After you've told them, back off. You're not going to pester anyone into being fine. You've probably known for much longer than they have. Also try to remember that the reason a lot of parents flip their weaves on finding out is that they're CONCERNED out of LOVE. Remember how I said that coming out is accepting a place in a persecuted minority. The fact of the matter is, identifying as LGBTQ+ is going to make your life a little bit harder...and no parent actively wants that for their kids.

Accept that they need their own time to accept your new identity. It may take minutes, days, months, or even years. They will come around in time. They stand to lose something hugely valuable if they don't: YOU. Remember, there are groups out there especially for LGBTQ+ youths. Should things go wrong, there is help out there (see "Build a Bridge" at the back of the book).

> I promised myself I would tell my parents if I ever had
> a boyfriend (I felt that being in a relationship and having
> to hide it was possibly the crappiest thing ever)—and
> so I did. I came out during the Easter holidays just
> after having been asked out by this boy. My parents
> were surprised and shocked—they hadn't suspected a
> thing—and it was weird talking about my gay feelings
> with them to start with, but over the past year we've all
> gotten more comfortable about it.
>
> —R, 17, London, UK

If you're ready to come out, congratulations! Now you've got your membership card, you're joining a legacy of people who've gone before, a sense of belonging, and queer culture—should you want it. The most important thing is that you are now free to be you AND shout about it from the rooftops. Or not—it's your choice.

COMING OUT AS TRANS

Coming out as LGB* is relatively easy compared with coming out as trans. Once you've come out, life pretty much carries on as normal. WHAT? THERE ISN'T A PARADE DOWN THE STREET?

No, I'm afraid not.

Coming out as trans requires more work. Situations vary wildly. Some young trans people have been dressing in clothes often assigned to the opposite gender since they were little kids. Some people have been doing so in secret or in a performance-based way as a drag queen or king.

You'll note that a lot of this crap wouldn't be necessary if society didn't have such closed ideas of what a man should dress like and what a woman should dress like.

When a person comes out as trans, it could mean admitting they sometimes like to cross-dress or that they intend to identify as their chosen gender full-time. As with sexuality, it's the admitting it aloud part that's terrifying. This time, however, people expect a physical transformation afterward.

The process is unique to every individual, but for people wishing to **transition** into a new gender full-time, there is a set plan. For most people, the first port of call a counselor— either one at your school or a professional therapist. That is not to say that being trans is a mental illness of itself, but when dealing with such a big step, it's important to establish it's the correct choice. The counselor will advise you on your options—there are a lot of things to think about and transitioning takes a long time. You may decide to go down a medical route and your counselor will guide you towards the right doctor.

If you've chosen to see a medical doctor and gotten a referral, you may well start on hormone treatment—for MTF patients, this involves taking estrogen, and for FTM, testosterone. The effects are sudden and, in some cases, irreversible.

It is important to seek medical help instead of self-administering hormones. The results are better. Period.

Hormones will change how you look and sound, but some trans people also opt for surgery. Some surgical procedures are covered by health insurance, but some have to be paid for privately (like facial feminization procedures). To have genital surgery (it's worth noting that a great many transgender people don't want genital surgery at all), most surgeons require you to have been living in your chosen gender for about two years.

Obviously, genital surgery is painful and the recovery period is lengthy, so some people choose to not have it. Others, however, feel they need a full physical overhaul.

It's very much about choice and understanding what's right for you.

One thing is for certain: If you or someone you know comes out as trans, the most important element is the new identity.

Choosing a name and making sure everyone uses the **correct pronouns** is as important as how you dress and look.

Won't Someone Think of the Children!

It can't have escaped your attention that the media is obsessed with the idea of transgender children right now. Some people have their panties in a right old bunch about it because apparently us powerful trans media types are brainwashing your people into having "sex changes."

Altogether now: LOLOLOLOLOLOLOLOLLOLOLOLOL times infinity.

Sure, Jan.

There is no such thing as "sex changes for kids." It doesn't happen. As mentioned, IF a young trans or nonbinary person WANTS medical interventions (many do not) they will likely be referred a specialist center for youth. Once there, they will have extensive counseling before POSSIBLY being prescribed a course of hormone blockers that DELAY the onset of puberty. All this means is that

IF that individual chooses to make a permanent physical change as a young adult, they won't then have to counteract the bodily consequences of puberty, i.e., breasts, a deeper voice, etc. It basically saves them a lot of time on a surgeon's table at a later date.

And that's ALL. No child is being whisked away for genital surgery, so can the panty-wringers please CHILL OUT? K thx bye.

IRENE'S STORY

Irene, 33, is an MTF transsexual from New Jersey.

> I opted for hormones, after taking some time to be sure I wanted this, because it had been my understanding that they are a very important medical step that can produce profound changes in body and mind. For some people, they're more important even than the things that we have to do through surgery, but I wouldn't go that far for myself.
>
> I'm given to understand that I personally am on the slower end of the scale of how fast changes tend to occur. I've been on hormone therapy for eighteen months now. It was quite exciting for the first couple months, and still is every time I notice some new progress. For a

while, I would measure my chest with a tape measure
to reassure myself that things were happening there. It
wasn't frightening at all; this has always been my fondest
desire, and it's a quite gentle process, really; there's
nothing to be scared by.

As far as what changed, the first thing I noticed was
that my nipples became developed—that is, stopped
being shriveled up like male ones are. Then, over about
three months, my hips widened, from thirty-two inches to
forty inches! I was still presenting as male at work during
that period, so that was a little difficult for me, since I
couldn't wear my actual wardrobe and had to find male
slacks that sort of fit.

Something should probably be said about facial-hair
removal, by the way. Hormones don't do that (nor do
they change the voice, which has to be done through
practice and often special training), so I had sessions for
that every weekend. There's a controversy about whether
laser treatment or electrolysis is better, which prevents
there being good advice in the community on it. The
facts are that laser covers many times more follicles per
session, while electrolysis is always permanent, even
on tough follicles. So what everybody winds up doing is
laser to get a clear face at first and electrolysis later on to
finish the job.

But nobody gave me this advice! So I just went for electrolysis, concurrently with starting hormones, because I didn't know any better. It was intensely painful, but I actually viewed that as a good thing, since it gave me some concrete sense of progress that I wasn't getting from the hormones at that time. Also, since most trans women (though I hardly knew any back then) have been through it at some point, there was a sense of belonging, which was nice.

For the first eight months or so, I had virtually no breast growth—enough that I could tell things had happened, with my shirt off, but it was quite distressing. They finally did start growing—I talked to my doctor and we played with my dosages a little—but I've never had the "growing pains" sensation that almost everybody mentions. As of today, I wear a B cup, but I don't really fill it.

I don't view that hormone therapy, nor the genital surgery that I am also seeking, as cosmetic at all; it's correcting a vital mismatch between body and soul. But the insurance company will see it that way on both counts (what could be less cosmetic than a complete change of genitalia?), so I'll be paying out of pocket.

I've spoken with other trans women on the subject, and most agree that there is an improved capacity to feel emotion. I can definitely confirm that in my own experience; it's too pronounced to be psychosomatic.

Frankly, I don't like the person who I was before starting hormones, and I never want to be that cold-hearted again. Also, I am able to summon tears when I feel the need, nowadays, which I never was before. Tears are very liberating.

In addition to increased emotionality, I had an almost immediate mood improvement. I had been depressed my whole life. For probably ten years prior to hormones, I was also deeply suicidal, making two very serious attempts—with subsequent hospitalizations. Once I got some estrogen in my system, I could no longer notice depressive "spiral" thinking patterns in myself. Even my psychiatrist saw a profound difference and ultimately took me off most of the psychiatric medications she had had me on, because, as we both agreed, they were no longer relevant to me. It was a complete turnaround, which is something that "just depression" patients never, ever experience. Beyond doubt, estrogen saved my life.

There are other aspects of transition which you didn't even tangentially ask about, so I won't go into them all, but just to name a few: There's the social side—telling one's friends (and, generally, losing most of them); telling one's family; losing any spouse and children that one might have. There's the clothing side, presenting as oneself regarding attire, hair, makeup, and so forth. There's the legal side, fighting with every single political and corporate entity that you had no idea even existed—I currently can't open a Verizon Internet service account in my new apartment because, in my new legal name, I have no credit history. Then there's the fact that, as a woman who plays video games, I face a hell of a lot of name-calling and hate speech from the twenty-something males who inhabit the same virtual spaces as me. And there's the fact that software development, my profession, is at least ninety-five percent male.

I wouldn't trade any of these problems for the world. I am so, so glad to have them.

CHAPTER 8

WHERE TO MEET PEOPLE LIKE YOU

Do you like the following things:

- Holding hands?
- Kissing?
- Picking the devil mushrooms off your pizza and giving them to someone else?
- Sex?
- Hugs?
- Watching TV while snuggling?
- The idea of any of these things?

If you answered yes to any of the above, then I'm afraid, sooner or later, you'll have to meet someone. You'll note that none of the activities are one-player games.

As previously mentioned, LGBTQ+ people are in a minority. MOST people identify as heterosexual, therefore finding someone the same gender as you who wants to hug and hold hands with you is a little bit tougher.

Clearly, being trans has nothing to do with your sexuality. Some trans people will be gay, others will be straight. Later in this chapter, we'll talk about the specific issues trans people might have when meeting someone.

You probably won't believe this but, once upon a time, gay men used to hang colored bandannas out of their back pockets to signal that they were gay and what kind of sexyfuntime they liked. Complicated much? Also, with rainbow-color hankies dangling from their pants, you can only imagine they looked like My Little Ponies.

Luckily, LGBTQ+ people have emerged from the shadows. The days of gay or bi people hiding away in unmarked subterranean bars and clubs are over (although those clubs do still exist and they serve a function, as we'll discuss later). We have trendy bars and hip clubs for the over twenty-one crowd, and websites, organizations, clubs, marches, and more for everyone—all designed to help us meet potential partners or friends.

THE LOOK OF LOVE

Ancient gay scholars (me and my friends) have often posited that there is a MYSTICAL SIXTH SENSE that allows homo-inclined people to sense when our own kind is close at hand. We are sex mediums, if you like: "There is a gay in this house... yes...yes, the presence is strong now...he's definitely a gay."

This gay radar became known as **GAYDAR**.

Of course, members of the LGBTQ+ community do not possess magical powers (or at least that's what we want regular people to think...). Instead, gaydar is a developed talent whereby we get good at reading body language.

How to hone your gaydar:

So you see someone you like the look of...

- The first step is CLOCK THE STEREOTYPES. As discussed, stereotypes are stereotypes for a reason, and some men and women do have a "gay look," probably BECAUSE we sometimes want to advertise ourselves to potential mates. A beardy guy wearing a leather harness IS likely to be gay (or a gladiator). Sadly, nearly all LGBTQ+ people are far more ambiguous than that, so we need further help.

- Look for SUSTAINED EYE CONTACT. This is by far the best gaydar at your disposal. I'm going to be super honest. Women (who I like an awful lot but do not like having sex with) mill around me all day. In passing, I might notice their super hair or something, but I don't really try to make eye contact. People, as a rule, make eye contact if they want to engage. If you see someone holding eye contact for much more than a second, or taking a second look, it's because they're trying to get your attention.

- INCREASED BODY CONTACT, such as a hand on your arm or shoulders, is another body language sign that someone is into you.

Very often, though, given that we're in the twenty-first century, most people just explain that they're gay. You could also just ask someone. How much easier is that?

These days a lot of younger LGBTQ+ people are out at school and college, so word spreads and you may well already know loads of other LGBTQ+ people already. Being LGBTQ+ isn't a big secret anymore for a lot of young people, so there's no need for special places to meet.

For others, though, adolescence and young adulthood can be an isolating time, and you may have to be a bit more proactive to find people like you.

SAFE SPACES

For a long time, homophobia and fear of verbal and physical assault was so bad that LGBTQ+ people did need special places where they could socialize free from intimidation. This is still somewhat true today. LGBTQ+ people are not zoo animals, and as such we do not like being stared at. It's depressing but true that even some quite well-meaning straight people find gay people to be a bit of a freak show.

Because of this, it's nice to go to places where you can meet new people without having to bother saying, "Sorry to ask this, but are you, like, erm...gay?" It saves SO much hassle.

This brings us to the concept of the **gay scene**, a somewhat out-of-date term which encompasses gay and bi men and women, and also trans people to some degree.

As discussed, being transgender has nothing to do with a person's sexuality, but transvestites, transsexuals, and drag queens have often sought refuge from gawkers in gay or lesbian bars or clubs—they're not ideal, but they're an accepting place.

A key problem with the gay scene is that nearly all bars and clubs are for twenty-one and over only—but we'll deal with that shortly.

SCENE QUEENS

Before we look at the various strands of the gay scene, it's important to stress that it's not for everyone. By that I don't mean heterosexual people, I mean US. Lots of LGBTQ+ people do not access "gay services" at all.

> I've never really had to engage with the gay scene because I've basically been in the same relationship my whole adult life. For me, I guess the gay scene may have had a slightly negative impact—I'd see all these people cross-dressing at gay pride events or big butch lesbians with French crops and very camp gay men dancing around, and I'd be like, "I'm not like that. I don't want to have to cut my hair short and spend the whole time talking about dildos and telling everyone about my sex life." It made me think that I was never going to quite fit in anywhere.
>
> It was quite a relief to discover that you can go out with someone of the same sex and then carry on with life as it was before, without having to make it central to your identity.
>
> —J, 28, Brighton, UK

Many LGBTQ+ people, especially those living in rural areas and smaller towns, will not have the same services that people in big cities (especially New York, San Francisco, and Vancouver) do. There is no rule that says all LGBTQ+ adults have to go to "gay clubs" or "gay bars."

THIS IS ANOTHER STEREOTYPE. Let's all throw sticks at it.

Gay people in Colorado probably like hiking. Gay people in California might enjoy surfing. Gay people in Vermont build snowmen.

Here's another thing—LGBTQ+ people IN big cities don't always access the gay scene either. It's very much a choice.

For some reason—possibly internalized homophobia—no one wants to admit to being a "scene queen," even people who do visit gay bars and clubs quite regularly. This is very silly.

However we live our lives, LGBTQ+ people have NOTHING to be ashamed of.

Let's not forget the benefits of having these safe spaces:

> Being a part of the gay scene allows you to meet people and make friends that have a lot of the same experiences and interests as you do. It is also a really good way to find potential romantic partners. The only way I met all of the girls I've dated was because I'm involved and active in the gay scene in my area. The disadvantages are that it can limit your worldview if you ONLY hang out with other gay

> people, and the dating scene can get a bit incestuous if you and all of your friends are fishing in the same dating pool.
>
> —Taylor, 23, U.S.

> Part of the reason I—a wee kid from Paisley in Scotland—moved south to London almost twenty years ago was because of the "gay scene" it promised.
>
> London was very good to me, and I had a lot of fun in my twenties and thirties there. The benefits were having easy access to many pubs and clubs where you could relax, be yourself, and, of course, meet ever-so-cute guys! It amazed me to be able to walk about in Soho holding hands with my boyfriend in public and not being laughed at, slagged off, or even attacked.
>
> —Aidy, 46, Margate, UK

It's also worth noting that the gay scene is probably more diverse than people give it credit for. There are as many stereotypes about the gay scene as there are about gay people.

CLUBS AND SOCIETIES

Obviously, you have to be over twenty-one to go to a bar or a club, and as not all LGBTQ+ people love drinking and partying anyway, there are an infinite variety of clubs and societies that allow people to hang out and meet each other. All parts of the gay scene are as much about meeting like-minded friends as they are finding a partner for sexyfuntime. A quick Google search will unearth gay book groups, gay cooking classes, singles nights, and just about every sort of fun activity you can shake a stick (I SAID STICK) at.

Erik, 34, London, is the chairperson of the London Gay Symphonic Winds—a group for LGBTQ+ (and also straight) musicians:

> Founded in 2005, the London Gay Symphonic Winds (LGSW), like many gay and lesbian groups, was formed to give people the opportunity to do something they enjoyed in a friendly and supportive environment without the fear of encountering prejudice. We have always been as much a social group as a musical one, and we aim to be as inclusive as possible without detriment to the musical standard. Because of our unique marriage of the social/musical goals, we have players of all ages, sexual orientation, and genders. The LGSW is a great way for people to meet friends outside of the regular bar and club scene.

For young LGBTQ+ people, there are specialist support groups at young people's centers around the country. A fabulous example in the UK is Allsorts Youth Project in Brighton, which gives support to young people living on the South Coast. If you talk to staff at your school or college or look online, I'm almost certain you'll find a similar LGBTQ+ youth group close-ish to where you live.

> I come [to a youth group] to interact with other LGBT people. There's help and advice if you're struggling with certain situations, like mental health or sexual health, and it's a nice, friendly atmosphere.
>
> —Lucy, 20 Brighton, UK

> I mainly come to socialize and meet new people, and they help with, like, if I got bullied at college for being gay there's people here that can help with that.
>
> —N, 17, Burgess Hill, UK

> I like coming to Allsorts because, being trans, I find there's not a lot of support out there, and there is a separate group here for trans people. It's nice to have a safe space.
>
> —Chezra, 19, Brighton, UK

As well as being a cool place to hang out and make friends like you, youth groups will also provide you with free condoms, lube, contraception, and advice. Please see a list of active youth groups at the back of the book.

It's also worth noting that pretty much every college and university in the country will have an LGBTQ+ group on campus.

These are a fantastic way to meet like-minded people and a great way to establish yourself away from home should you go on to higher education. Each year cities all over the world celebrate with gay pride parades; people from the LGBTQ+ community come out and celebrate while showing their support for equality and awareness. It's a great event to attend with friends from school while creating connections within the community. These parades take place at the end of June each year to commemorate the Stonewall Riots that started on June 28, 1969 in New York City. These riots sparked the formation of activist groups that began to heavily influence LGBTQ+ rights in the U.S. for years to come.

There are also specialized group support meetings for trans people and those who may be thinking of transitioning. (See "Helpful Numbers and Websites and Stuff" at the back of the book.)

BARS AND NIGHTCLUBS

If you live in the U.S. and are over twenty-one or live in

Canada and are over eighteen, you are very lucky because you are old enough to get into your local "gay bar" or "gay club." Again, these are catch-all terms that can also include "girl bars" for gay women. Some establishments are for (or will run special nights for) cross-dressers, transsexuals, and transvestites.

These places are not to everyone's taste (and again, they only cater to those who are legal), although gay scenes in cities are more diverse and so cater to broader tastes. Issues range from the music...

> [The gay scene] is great if you like sugary drinks and bubble gum pop.
>
> —Stuart, 33, Brighton, UK

to the clientele...

> There are a lot of nasty, bitter queens around most scenes.
>
> —Dani, 29, Newcastle upon Tyne, UK

BUT the role of the gay bar is historical. As mentioned before, they provide safe spaces for LGBTQ+ people to meet free from ridicule or harassment.

People use gay bars and clubs in a variety of ways:

- **To have a good time.** Whatever music you're into, there's a bar or club for you somewhere. You can go with your friends and dance your little gay socks off.
- **To meet new friends.** Contrary to popular belief, gay and bi people don't always (a.) get it on or (b.) scratch each other's eyes out on first contact. It is nice to have friends who understand what it's like to be LGBTQ+, because we all have some shared experiences (e.g., coming out, the hilarity of Grindr).
- **Sex.** LGBTQ+ people cannot claim a monopoly on this one. Up and down the country, EVERYONE is going out to clubs to make out and perhaps something more. It's the human mating dance, and we do it to David Guetta in sweaty underground lairs.

HOW TO FLIRT

1. Make eye contact. If prolonged eye contact is held, you can assume they're interested.

2. Approach. Start with "Hey," "Hi," or "Hello." If you're abroad, you may have to revise this strategy.

3. If they respond positively, ask if they would like a drink. (If you and they are of age and drinks are available.)

4. Chat! Compliment! Dance! When complimenting, always choose nonarbitrary things—things they chose, like their clothes.

5. If the time is right, move in a little closer. If that feels right, you could perhaps give a little kiss a go too.

Most major towns and cities will have at least ONE gay bar or gay club. This is why rural LGBTQ+ people often relocate to places with a gay scene. But no one is forcing you to. There are loads of other ways you can meet people if you don't like bars and clubs (or are too young to go).

It goes without saying that not everyone you find attractive will also find you attractive. It's that simple. Not everyone is to your taste, so you won't always be to someone else's. If you get rejected by someone you like, never take it personally—you're just not their type, and that's their problem, not yours.

> I met my boyfriend in a nightclub in Clapham. I'd seen
> him there before, and we just started smiling and saying
> hi when we saw each other. One night I saw him standing
> by himself, so I just went over and talked to him. We did
> have a bit of a snog, but we both had friends staying over,
> so that was as far as it went. I got his number and we
> arranged to go on a date the week after.
>
> —Jamie, 28, London, UK

FAQ: Why is the gay scene so druggie? That stereo-type isn't especially fair because what club scene isn't? Clubbing and recreational drug use go hand in hand, and I assure you straight clubs are just as druggie, but it can be surprising to see guys (or indeed girls) in their forties and fifties off their rockers on plant fertilizer every Saturday. Maybe it's because most gay people don't have kids back home and so can go a little wild. Maybe it's because we're antiestablishment. Maybe it's because we have a terrible Peter Pan complex and we need to grow up.

Just because it's commonplace doesn't mean it's RIGHT, SENSIBLE, or LEGAL. Drug use is none of those things. With drugs, as with sex, it's ALWAYS your CHOICE. No one is forcing anyone to take drugs on the gay scene.

You might have seen reports on the so-called "chemsex" scene. This is (usually) gay men getting high together for sexyfuntime. Again, this isn't anything new, but cases of drug-related deaths have raised concern. The most important thing is your safety. The problem with mixing drugs and sex is that common sense and safety often fly out the window. By all means, have fun, but no sex and no drug is worth putting your health and safety on the line for. You're worth more than that (*shampoo ad hair flick*).

Beware: Illegal drugs are clearly dodgy at best, deadly at worst, and you could wind up with a criminal record. St Thomas's Hospital in London now charges some gay clubs a levy because of the number of casualties being wheeled off the dance floor on a stretcher. Not sexy.

MUTUAL FRIENDS

I think this one is possibly the best path to finding a suitable partner. What could be better than having your friends vet potential suitors like Sex Factor judges: "No, you aren't going through to the next round." "You're going through to LIVE DATES! Congratulations!" etc.

Being set up is often fantastic but also a potential 'mare of Elm Street proportions. PARTICULARLY when you first come out, well-meaning people (often straight) will bombard you with "OOOOH, I KNOW A GAY GUY/GIRL— YOU SHOULD MARRY HIM/HER!" It is a sad fact that many straight people think having "gay" in common is the stuff true love is made of. It isn't.

Other LGBTQ+ friends or friends who know you well, however, can be fantastic matchmakers, especially once they know your type. A lot of people throw house parties especially to mingle and mix their single pals and hopefully get you to bring some spare parts too!

Laura, 21, an MTF trans girl, and her partner started out as friends:

> I first met Tess back in 2008. When we met, I was still living as male and in total denial about why I was so depressed all the time. We met when she and her group of friends came into the sweet shop where I worked, and we hit it off right away. We started talking because she was a huge fan of the band whose shirt I was wearing. We met up after work to hang out, and we very quickly became close friends, but we were never romantically linked. We knew what we felt was not attraction but friendship.
>
> Skip ahead a few years and my gender dysphoria had hit its peak. I was near suicidal over the changes happening to my body, and I just didn't want to face the reality that I couldn't face living the life I was living much longer. So I turned to Tess. She was the first person I

came out to about my feelings of dysphoria, and she was hugely supportive, helping me find resources and generally being there for me during the earliest stages of my transition.

She was there during my trying to decide on a new name, my awkward first attempts at presenting as female and my first times going out in public as Laura, all the while standing by my side, proud to know me, proud to be a part of the time in my life when most trans allies are most hesitant. She was the first person to switch to referring to me only by my new name, the first to put her support behind me, and she stuck by my side throughout it all.

Tess is gay. In the time I'd known her, she had only ever dated women. I knew she had dated men before, but since she first dated a woman, she had never turned back. As I transitioned, our relationship began to shift too. It became clear that while neither of us had been interested in a heterosexual relationship with each other, we were interested in each other as I progressed through my transition. I know a lot of my hang-ups about relationships had been due to my deep hatred of my old body and the fact I didn't find heterosexual relationships arousing. Coming out and starting to allow myself some freedom with who I was completely opened me up to the prospect of being attracted to and in love with someone.

As I transitioned Tess started to see me as someone she found attractive too. What had been a great friendship, with sudden romantic and sexual feelings developing, didn't take long to turn into us starting to date. Two years later, we're still going strong, happier than ever and looking forward to whatever the future holds. She has been incredibly respectful of my boundaries regarding my body and has stuck by my side through everything, reminding me that someone in this world thinks I'm beautiful, even when I don't.

ONLINE

We live our lives online. It makes sense therefore that the social part of social media involves meeting new friends and potential partners. I don't know anyone who HASN'T had someone slide into their DMs. Be mindful, though, that there are age limits on most social media platforms.

Some websites are set up especially for dating—however you identify—and they're all designed to help people meet each other for romance, dating, or sex.

Tips for Online Dating

- NEVER put personal information such as your address or telephone number on the web (unless you like being murdered).
- It's polite to present a clear, recent face picture. And don't cheat with airbrushed photos!
- If you decide to meet someone, arrange a date in a brightly lit café or bar, not stabby alleyway.
- Some people arrange to meet at their houses—be aware that, if you do this, you are inviting strangers into YOUR HOME. This is never a hundred percent safe.
- Be aware that many dating sites have a minimum age of eighteen, although some people arrange dates through Twitter or Facebook too.

I've had dates (and consequently sex) with people I've met through Twitter, but they've come along as a result of my normal interactions on there rather than anything deliberate. Facebook is different—that's reserved for people I actually "know."

—Luke, 28, London, UK

APPS

The smartphone revolution understood that, like anything in the twenty-first century, we'd eventually want to be able to download sex. It wouldn't surprise me if, in a couple of years, we can download the idea of sex so convincingly that we won't have to bother with the messy bodily fluids and pesky emotional stuff at all.

It is a fact that although grown-up adult types are sometimes looking for a serious relationship, sometimes they are just looking for a spot of sexyfuntime. You may come to establish that gay and bi men in particular do seem to quite like sex. OK, nearly everyone likes sex, but gay guys really seem to have cornered the market. Remember, this is fine as long as you're honest and always use a condom. Gay and bi men have taken to app sex like ducks to sexy water.

Technology changes frighteningly quickly (the lesbian app Qrushr has been and gone already), but it seems that market leader, Grindr, is here to stay. **Note: Grindr also has an age minimum age of eighteen years old.**

How Sex Apps Work:

1. Upload a tiny pic of yourself to the app.
2. The app works out your location.

3. The app tells you who the nearest homosexuals are.
4. You then chat to them.
5. Because they are near, it is easy to meet up with them.

NOW. *Not* everyone on a sex app is there for sex. Like a website, it's just another way to meet like-minded guys or girls (there ARE lesbian versions out there). Once again, the app removes the need to ask, "Hey! You over there with the arms! You gay?"

If you want to use a sex app for chatting or dates, be VERY clear about this. In this instance, posting a pic of your nekkid chest would be somewhat misleading, no? Similarly, if you're looking for the ubiquitous "fun" (the words "sex," "shag," and the F-word, ironically, are banned on most sex apps), be upfront about it and then no one's feelings are going to get hurt.

Most of us know at least one loving couple who met on a sex app and it became something more, but I'd politely suggest that downloading a sex app to find a committed partner is a little like going to KFC for a healthy meal—literally fruitless.

THE GREAT SEX APP DEBATE

Pro Sex App

> I have used Grindr—the advantages are you can get what you want quickly. The downside is that its the same people repeatedly, so can get boring very quickly, and there is an awful lot of "Hi, how are you?", which people could do without. I prefer to be more forward in those scenarios.
>
> —Jonny, London, UK

> The benefits are obvious: quick, easy, and uncomplicated sex. On the downside, you always find the same people online whenever you're at home, and it matches you with people solely on the basis of proximity—so the chances of meeting someone with whom you have more than a physical connection is very slim.
>
> —Luke, 28, London, UK

> I've met a variety of interesting people through [sex apps]. They are predominantly used for sex though. They're sold to us as "social networking" apps, but we all know what they're really for. It's a bit like selling a dildo under the pretext that it's sole use is a draft excluder. I don't have a problem with that aspect of it—if people

> want casual sex, then something like Grindr is a must—
> but I've met quite a few new friends through it, so like
> anything I suppose it's what you decide to make of it.
>
> —Stuart, 34, Brighton, UK

Another major plus to sex apps is they allow a degree of anonymity, so guys and girls who aren't out can meet people this way without having to self-identify by entering a gay bar.

Anti Sex App

> I've downloaded Grindr and chatted/sexted men on it
> but have never physically met men via it. If one was in
> need of a sexual encounter, whether it be a hookup or
> something less casual, one could almost always find
> something. However, the men on these apps tend to
> be shallow when it comes to appearances and sexual
> identity (i.e., "looking for masc," "white and Asian only.")
>
> —Anon, 20, Minneapolis, Minnesota

> I know one guy who got gonorrhea, chlamydia, and
> syphilis from some guy he met on Grindr. All in one go,
> like a three-for-two special.
>
> —Ryan, 32, New Jersey

> After a long and slightly messy breakup, I briefly used Grindr and Scruff—thinking that it would be an easy way of meeting a potential boyfriend...I realized very quickly that these services are mainly tailored toward enabling like-minded people to have sexual encounters—which isn't what I was looking for.
>
> —Mike, London, UK

> I don't believe there are any advantages to these apps. I believe they are unsafe.
>
> —Mica, 23, London, UK

Using a sex app to hook up is LITTERED with potential risks for which the makers take no responsibility. Tucked away on the websites of sex apps (in very small print) is a safety section which advises users to make sensible "dating" choices. Yes, everyone on Grindr is looking for a good, hard date.

In order to have the sex off a sex app you will have to meet a potential partner, so this means them coming to yours or you going to theirs. Obviously, this is very risky indeed.

As mentioned above, the anonymity of sex-app users means that they have become colonies of cheating partners—a hive of shitweasels, if you will. Beware faceless profiles. They're faceless for a reason.

Some Sex App Tips

- Include a picture of yourself. Don't steal other people's. That's weird and shady.
- If you don't include a face pic, expect the first message anyone EVER sends you to be "PIC?"
- On the same subject, if you think your key selling point is your bare chest, we're in bother. Don't be a **prawn**—"great body, but I wouldn't eat the head."
- If you don't give your age, weight, and height, people will assume you're old, fat, and tiny.
- As regards all "sexting," sharing pictures of your bits is not a great idea. Things do get shared around. Use common sense.
- If you're THAT HORNY that you want to do a "sex meet," meet the "trick" in a public place for a drink first. That way you can assess if you fancy them in the flesh/they are not a twitchy-eyed freakazoid before letting them into your house. This is much, MUCH safer, obviously.
- You can ALWAYS say NO. If someone from a sex app turns up and you don't like the look of them, don't be scared to turn them away at the door (of the safe, public venue you chose to meet at). Awkward, yes, but better than awkward sex.

- This one goes without saying, but ALWAYS WEAR A CONDOM.
- If you are on Grindr, under the age of eighteen (it happens), be aware that swapping "adult" pics is actually illegal—you are distributing child pornography, even if it's of yourself.

DATING SAME-SEX PEOPLE

To revert to well-worn stereotypes, gay men are quick to jump into bed and gay women are quick to move in together, but as gay is now thoroughly mainstream, it seems likely that at some point you'll want to "date" away from underground sex dungeons and drag shows.

Once you've met someone, be it in the street, bar, club, or sex app, you'll need to get to know them better. How does one go about this? Like most people, it's all about wining and dining. Getting to know someone is vital because the outside package, however gorgeous, isn't going to sustain your interest for very long.*

---

* Excluding Jake Gyllenhaal. I could merely look at him until the end of time.

DATE IDEAS

Restaurant	Theater	Exhibition	Sightseeing
Recital	Museum	Walk/hike	Concert
Bike ride	Sailing	Bowling	Gym
Picnic	Drinks/cocktails	Paint a mug	Movie
Shopping	Miniature golf	Coffee	Wine tasting

Those are but twenty suggestions—feel free to invent your own. I think the ones where you DO STUFF, like an exhibition or a concert, are the BEST because then you have something to talk about right in front of you. Early dates can be tricky because at first you might not have any shared contacts, so it becomes a bit of a job interview, with each person presenting facts about their life.

That said, dating is so important to establish if there's anything in the pretty packaging that you like. This can take weeks, even months. There's no rush. The goal of dating is to establish if the person you're seeing is a keeper.

Who Pays on a Gay Date (or Gayte, If You Will)?

For heterosexual people, this one is curiously medieval—the guy always offers to pay unless he is awful.

But what if it's two guys or two girls? Generosity is mega sexy, so I think it's always nice to offer to pay. Your partner will probably say, "Don't be silly—let's split the bill." This is usually the way it goes.

If it was a good date and you'd like another, you can always say, "Well, you get this and I'll get the next one..."

If you're in a food situation and your partner starts working out exactly what each person owes, dump them at once.

TRANS DATING

This is complicated. Clearly, a trans person can also be gay or bi, so some of the information in the previous sections is relevant, but some trans people will identify as straight. Being trans can be a complication in new relationships, but it isn't always. Many partners are fully accepting of the situation because they have fallen for YOU, not your genitals! Many transsexuals are supported through transition by new or existing partners. Other people are specifically attracted to trans men or women.

Worrying about finding a boyfriend or girlfriend should never be a barrier that stops a person changing their gender. It's much more important to be who you truly are than to be in a relationship. When you are happy and content, you'll attract far more partners anyway!

Jane of Washington, DC, is a trans woman who dates mostly women:

> [I use] almost exclusively OKCupid. The reason for this is that it allows me to "screen" people who have an issue with transgender people. OKCupid has a specific question, "Would you date a person who has had a gender change?" and another, "At what time is it appropriate for a transgender person to reveal their gender status?"

I don't know what ANYONE did before the Internet, but there are now a plethora of online dating sites especially for trans people, although, once more, you have to be over eighteen to access most of them.

Duncan is a trans man from Jackson, Mississippi:

> Being comfortable with myself and being fully open about my trans status means that I end up dating people who are really interested in me. And if me being

trans scares them off, we probably didn't need to date anyway.

Truthfully most of [my] post-transition dating experiences have been positive. The only negative things haven't had anything to do with being trans, but rather just not being compatible with someone.

Harrison from the UK identifies as trans bisexual:

Personally I find dating has been easier since I came out as trans. I am always honest, which I think is something I personally desire in a relationship, regardless of gender or sexuality. I found, after I came out, I was more confident in approaching people and even that it intrigued a lot of people. Some friends have admitted to questioning their own sexuality because of meeting trans people and the possibility of dating someone LGBTQ.

The only negative experience dating as a trans man I had was that the person I was dating when I came out— who identified as bisexual—had a negative reaction. While I don't count it as a loss, I came to understand that I needed to be with a partner that would respect me for my lifestyle and that I wanted to transition. At the end of the day I am transitioning for myself and no one else!

CHAPTER 9

THE INS AND OUTS OF GAY SEX

This chapter is about sex. Therefore it has sex in it. WELL, DUH. If you are a younger reader and feel you aren't ready for the finer details of same-sex pairings, then simply skip this whole chapter.

HOWEVER, before you do, I'd like to remind you that we taught you all about straight sex when you were ELEVEN YEARS OLD during sixth grade. The fact that they didn't also teach you what same-sex couples do is nothing less than institutionalized homophobia. Straight sex was presented as the norm to make five percent of the population feel abnormal. Is there something icky about gay sex? Is there something wrong with it? I challenge any politician to discuss this with me. I WILL RUIN THEM.

This chapter is simply all the stuff teachers SHOULD be saying if they want to be inclusive of people with same-sex feelings.

When I was tiny, the idea of two men or two women having sex was hilariously funny. I ascertained at quite a young age that a boy had to pop his peen inside a lady-locket in order to make a baby happen. That made sense. What didn't make sense was how two men could possibly enjoy making the ends of their penises meet in the middle, or what joy two women could garner from rubbing their front bums together. Surely the friction alone would spark a small fire.

I, for real, used to think that

"bumming" was the act of bouncing bottoms together like a fleshy pillow fight. I was confused at how such a wholesome activity could cause such outrage and disdain.

My confusion, I'm sure you'll agree, was delightfully innocent but actually hinted at something much darker.

Once upon a time, there was a very bad lady—let's, for the sake of argument, call her Maggie. She decreed that teachers in the UK must not include "gay lifestyles" in sex education lessons.

This was called "Section 28," and it explains why I had no clue what same-sex couples did to get each other off.

Some years later, a slightly less evil man—let's call him Tony—took this piece of legislation away. That was good because now teachers COULD talk about being gay in schools.

Only one problem: Lots still didn't because they weren't told exactly what they should say to young people. Teachers aren't given scripts. Very often, teachers still sidestep the subject entirely because they're scared they're being "inappropriate." How can teaching THOUSANDS of young LGBTQ+ people in schools how to have safe, healthy sexual relationships be "inappropriate?"

> My school was deeply conservative, and the entire extent of our sex education was to shock us out of

> sexual behavior by showing us stacks of photographs of
> diseased genitalia. Somehow this didn't violate their "no
> pornography" policy; maybe it doesn't count as porn if the
> sight of it makes you want to dry-retch. The existence of
> LGBTQ+ people was ignored.
>
> —Stephen, 22, Johannesburg, South Africa

Lucky for the UNIVERSE, therefore, that I have no shame and will happily fill you in on all the ins and outs of "gay sex."

A WORD ON PORN

> My earliest sexual experiences were some of the most
> scary, embarrassing, nightmare-inducing incidents I
> dread to think about. I was so unprepared. You think
> watching as much porn as your eyes can take will help—
> believe me, it doesn't.
>
> —James, 20, London, UK

Let's get one thing straight: Pornography is NOT sex education. That is true of all porn—gay, straight, lesbian, whatever.

Here's why:

1. Porn stars are expert sex-doers. No one expects you to be able to do that—especially not when you're learning.

2. Porn doesn't reflect real life. If men in the army were having as much sex as gay porn suggests, the world would be in great peril.

3. Porn stars are selected on the basis of their fantastic bodies, huge willies, and fake boobs. Not many people look like that in real life.

4. If all gay women really had fingernails that long, emergency rooms would be a lot busier with all the clit injuries.

5. No one is using condoms. You must always wear a condom.

Basically, porn is fine and fun, but it is in no way REAL. You can take ideas, but it's definitely not for beginners. Everyone, including young gay, lesbian, bi, curious, and queer people, is entitled to high-quality, expertly taught sex education.

"GAY VIRGINITY"

Heterosexual sex is taught as THE NORM. Not just at school but in 99 percent of TV shows, films, books, magazines, and news stories. It's no wonder, therefore, that many LGBTQ+ people's first sexual dalliances are with the opposite sex. Ah, the feeling of being shoehorned into societal norms. Cozy.

Therefore, many LGBTQ+ people lose their virginity twice—once with each gender! Both can be equally nerve-racking, but this is how a lot of people figure out what their preference is.

> With a guy it was awkward. I didn't know what I was doing or what anything was supposed to feel like. I was really disconnected from myself. With a girl, it was exciting; it was comfortable. It helped that we were each other's first girl experience, so neither one of us really knew what we were doing. But we learned quickly, and it was just fun.
>
> —Sarah, 29, Iowa

> I lost my virginity at age sixteen. I was making a concerted effort at the time to prove to myself that I was a hetero male so that I could ignore my thoughts, and my attraction to women was all I had to cling to on that front. I quickly realized that while I was attracted to women, I wasn't attracted to them as a man; I was attracted to them as a woman, in a purely female sense. I like to view my losing my "gay virginity" at age twenty, last year. This was the first time I had sex with a partner who

viewed me as female, viewed us as a gay couple, and was willing to work with me to have sex in a way that felt appropriate for me. This was the first time I had sex as a woman in my eyes and my partner's, which feels a much more real event to me.

—Laura, 21, UK

On my sixteenth birthday, I went to hang out at a guitar shop near my house which I used to spend a lot of time at. The owner was older and married, and we'd been flirting with each other for a few months, though till then nothing had come of it. On this day, however, I spent hours there, as I had nothing to do till my mom finished work. The shop was quiet, and as the morning went on we got more and more tactile until we were rubbing our crotches against each other. We managed to stop short of getting our knobs out in the shop, and he suggested that I come round to his house the next day on his day off when his wife would be at work to help him "wash his car." When I arrived, the car had already been washed, though it took us both a couple of hours to muster up the courage to do anything. In the meantime, we made excruciating small talk and browsed that week's Lidl leaflet. We carried on seeing each other for a few months.

—L, 28, Brighton, UK

PART ONE: BOY-ON-BOY SEX

Here is a diagram of a cisgender boy. If you are also a boy, you are probably aware which parts FEEL NICE when you touch them, but here's a rough guide. Trans men may have slightly different bodies.

Lips: Sex should always start with a kiss. Initially, you might not go any further than a kiss, in fact. Kissing is as intimate as sex, and if you're not comfortable going further than a kiss, a good partner will respect this and wait.

Neck/Ears: These sensitive areas love being kissed and licked.

Skin: Any part of your body will respond to being stroked and kissed.

Nipples: A lot of guys like having their nipples played with. They are mega sensitive.

Penis If you are a guy, you'll already know that even a gentle spring breeze can be enough to inspire a stiffy in this super-sensitive organ. But keep in mind that sex doesn't begin and end with your dick. Be creative.

Testicles: Also to be treated with loving care.

A BLOKE

Bum: Up your bum you have a prostate gland which feels nice when massaged. The anus is also sensitive and responds to being played with.

Doing the Sex

Two cisgender men can pleasure each other in a variety of fun ways.

Handies

Perhaps the most important skill you will master as a gay or bi man is the timeless classic, the hand job. The good news is, you can practice on yourself. The bad news is, each guy has become very used to his own way of getting himself off. Learning how to find a partner's personal style can take ages, but it can be very rewarding when you do.

Something they don't teach you in school is that, in order to be able to cum at all, you or your partner may need to finish off with a handie. A lot of people find it hard to cum through other types of sex. This is fine, and certainly not something you have to apologize for.

A GOOD HANDIE is all about the wrist action. Rub the head of his cock back and forth with your hand. Try different speeds and pressures until he responds positively.

A BAD HANDIE is grasping a penis and shaking it like a ketchup bottle.

Finally, my misunderstanding about rubbing two peens together wasn't far off the mark—rubbing them together in one hand feels awesome—MEGA COMBOHANDIE (trademark pending).

TIP: If your partner is circumcised ("cut") you will want to try a drop of lube—remember he hasn't got as much skin to move around as uncut guys.

Blowies

Oral sex is popping another dude's peen in your mouth or, indeed, popping yours in his. There is only one hard and fast rule when it comes to blow jobs—WATCH THE TEETH. Lips and tongue, yes; teeth, NO.

As with hand jobs and breakfast eggs, all men like their blow jobs served in different ways. The term "blow job" is massively misleading, as you won't actually be blowing on his penis—it's more about sucking (although I stress you're not trying to suck his kidneys out through his urethra). It's more about sliding your mouth up and down the shaft of his cock.

Letting a guy cum in your mouth is a safe sex no-no. Get away from the volcano before it erupts. In fact, be aware that many sexually transmitted infections (STIs) are often spread through oral sex.

Bumming

It is a universal truth that many men like sticking their willies inside things. I suspect it must be biological. Well, in the absence of a vagina, gay and bi men make excellent use of the back door.

Wanna know a secret? Straight people have anal sex all the time too. Another one? Straight men like stuff up their bums just as much as gay ones. Why? As mentioned before, the prostate gland (located just up your bum) feels amazing when massaged. Lots of men, gay or straight, like how this feels. Anal sex ISN'T a "gay thing."

Still, unlike vaginal sex, a little more thought has to go into anal sex, and here's why:

Pre-care: As pleasant as bumming can be, we must hold in mind that the primary function of the back passage is to do poos. Poo is not sexy. Therefore, those of you planning to have anal sex will need to dedicate a portion of time to ensuring poo doesn't creep into sexyfuntime.

The best, healthiest method is to make sure you've been to the bathroom before attempting butt sex and have had a jolly good clean afterward. Poo is not held in the rectum, so there shouldn't be an issue. Some people choose to douche. You can buy a douche online or from an adult shop. Basically, this involves squirting a little bit of water into your back passage to clean the area out. It's a DIY colonic irrigation!

It goes like this: Squirt the lukewarm water up your bum, hold for a few moments before releasing into the toilet. Repeat this process two or three times or until the water runs clear. Note: This water is not drinking water.

A lot of people don't douche. For one thing it's not very spontaneous, and for another some sources suggest more harm than good can come from washing away the butt hole's mucus lining (which protects the bum lining from tearing, thus preventing some STIs).

I recognize this doesn't sound VERY sexy, but this is the reality of butt sex, I'm afraid, and a little forethought will make your sex sexier.

Roles: This is where dude–dude pairings can get tricky. At the end of the day, if you want to have anal sex, one of you is going to have to go "top" (the one who puts his willy in) and the other "bottom" (the one who gets the willy up his bum). Gay men seem to spend a lot of time talking about this. It's actually not a massive deal, as most guys are "versatile" and will happily switch roles depending on mood, although there are guys who prefer to be strictly top or bottom.

Is the top "the man" and the bottom "the woman"?

NO. The whole point of being gay is that it's two guys. Being a bottom makes a dude no less manly than his top partner. Look at it this way: He's literally "taking it like a man."

How do you know if you're a top or bottom? It's easy—if the thought of having a big hard thing poked up your tush is arousing, you are probably a bottom.

See? Easy.

Some guys are quite up-front about their preference, as this saves time further down the line and the potential awkwardness of winding up in bed with two confirmed tops desperately trying to convince each other why they might like to think otherwise. That said, most of the time, this can be figured out as you go along and, as mentioned above, there's no rule that says you have to have anal sex every time you have sex. Far from it.

Lube: Unlike the vagina, the anus does NOT lubricate itself. You NEED lube if you're going to attempt anal. This is for two reasons. One, anal sex hurts. The anus does not have the capacity to stretch in the same way a vagina does. This means it's a tight hole (which feels nice for the top), but it also means it can be **very** uncomfortable for the bottom. This is why lots of men don't like being bottom. With the right **water-based** lube, however, it can be hugely enjoyable—a good kind of pain like a deep tissue massage.

Two, lube makes it less likely your condom will split. The anus is a pretty fragile membrane, which means it's easier to get STIs through anal sex than vaginal. You really do **need** to wear a condom for anal sex.

P.S. A bit of spit, *Brokeback Mountain*-style, is NOT a substitute for a proper water-based lubricant, which you can get free with condoms from gay bars, doctors and clinics, or buy pretty much anywhere. Vaseline and baby oil are oil-based and actually decay condoms. Don't use these as lube.

Finally, it's worth noting that some gay and bi men don't like anal sex at all. It could be that it kinda hurts, or it could be the fact that it's the hole poo comes out of, but some guys (and girls) just don't go there, and that's fine. NOT having bum fun doesn't mean you can't identify as a gay man, OBVIOUSLY.

PART TWO: GIRL-ON-GIRL SEX

Here is a diagram of a cisgender woman. If you are also a woman, you are probably aware which parts FEEL NICE when you touch them, but here's a rough guide. Trans women may have slightly different bodies.

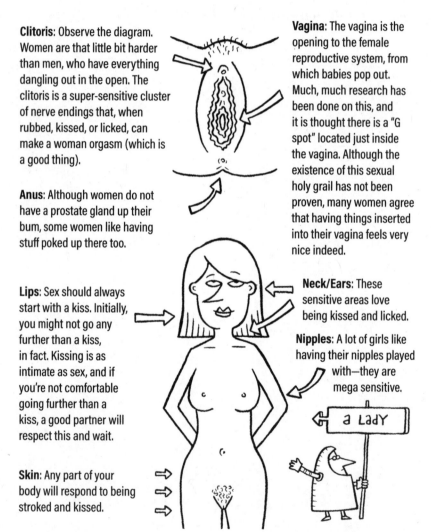

Clitoris: Observe the diagram. Women are that little bit harder than men, who have everything dangling out in the open. The clitoris is a super-sensitive cluster of nerve endings that, when rubbed, kissed, or licked, can make a woman orgasm (which is a good thing).

Anus: Although women do not have a prostate gland up their bum, some women like having stuff poked up there too.

Lips: Sex should always start with a kiss. Initially, you might not go any further than a kiss, in fact. Kissing is as intimate as sex, and if you're not comfortable going further than a kiss, a good partner will respect this and wait.

Skin: Any part of your body will respond to being stroked and kissed.

Vagina: The vagina is the opening to the female reproductive system, from which babies pop out. Much, much research has been done on this, and it is thought there is a "G spot" located just inside the vagina. Although the existence of this sexual holy grail has not been proven, many women agree that having things inserted into their vagina feels very nice indeed.

Neck/Ears: These sensitive areas love being kissed and licked.

Nipples: A lot of girls like having their nipples played with—they are mega sensitive.

a LadY

DOING THE SEX

Two women can pleasure each other in a variety of fun ways.

Fingers

Far more effective than a penis in many ways, a hand can do the job of five penises. When gay women refer to having sex, this is usually what they mean. Lesbians can stimulate the clitoris and vagina and bring their partner to orgasm with their fingers; sometimes both partners can do this simultaneously.

Oral

That clitoris really does like being licked and kissed. Again, girls can take it in turns to perform oral sex or, if feeling adventurous, they can perform it at the same time.

Toys and Strap-Ons

Some women like these; some don't. Much has been written about why gay women would seek to play with a replacement penis, but I say who the heck cares—if it feels nice, go for it! Moreover, a man is more than a penis—just because a woman wants something a bit penis-shaped doesn't mean she fancies broad-shouldered, beardy, no-boobed men.

Toys, dildos, vibrators, and strap-ons all fulfill the same purpose—a prosthesis to insert into the vagina. As with gay men, one woman isn't the "man." Two women having same-sex sex are both (yup) women!

Don't Take It from Me

Clearly, I am not a gay woman and, as such, why would you possibly come to me for tips on girl-girl sex? Well, quite. So I've called in an expert—gay writer, Fi Locke:

Let's talk about dildos: I think a lot of people assume that where there is no penis, a desperate sexual void is created, out of which something dick shaped must ultimately slot in order to satisfy a vagina.

Basically, there's holes everywhere, but you DON'T HAVE TO FILL THEM ALL! Not necessarily even with your tongue (personally, I don't think that feels nice) and not with something penis-shaped either.

I think most good orgasms revolve around the clit—well, for me and mine anyway! If you then want to get a bit fancy, there's nothing wrong with a few fingers inside (or a hand, depending on, well...y'know) during or proceeding on from some clitoral stimulation.

But that's orgasms. And as great as they are, it's not always all about them.

I've only ever slept with two women who enjoyed using dildos. I hate wearing a strap-on. I've only ever done it once and

NEVER AGAIN! But then I'm more of a receiving kind of person anyway. (Also, strap-ons are really hard work! You need to be FIT to really shag with one of them! And don't ever expect to cum when you're wearing it.)

The whole "butch dykes love strap-ons" thing is rubbish. I've heard differing opinions from friends and lovers about this, which vary from agreement with the above statement to actually feeling quite emasculated by a "pretend dick." It's totally personal. Some people love them, some people don't.

But back to orgasms. I love a good shag from a hand or a dildo—vaginal or anal—but, honestly, that's not about the orgasm; it's about the pleasure of being shagged. And sometimes that pleasure is pleasure enough in itself. That's not a timid "It's ok darling, as long as you're happy, I'm happy" excuse. Genuinely, there doesn't always need to be an orgasm.

What else? Well, it's OK to ask for help sometimes. Everybody's lady gardens are mapped out differently, so if your lover is doing it wrong, help her out. Even if it means doing it for her once or twice. That might feel like you're just using her hand to have a wank with, and it is, really, but hopefully after a while she'll start to notice where you're putting it.

I've been with a lot of girls with this kind of "This isn't straight sex, it's lesbian sex, and we're nicer and more respectful than them" attitude. That's boring. It's really boring. Just go for it and don't ever be ashamed about anything.

Lastly, I think you'll always have to take turns (unless you're 69ing). I haven't found an effective way to not take turns yet. Just make sure you don't do it in a "Right, I suppose I have to do you, now" kind of way.

Actually, really lastly: On reflection, I don't think girl-on-girl sex is any different to any other type of sex. If you just listen to what your body wants, what turns you on, and are never ashamed to ask for it, and if you experiment wherever possible, explore every corner of your desire, even if you only do it once, then you'll learn what you love and what you don't want and, voilà, you'll be enjoying sexy sex in no time!

Oh, okay, actual last thoughts:

1. *Why do they always put "veins" on dildos? It's gross.*
2. *Note to manufacturers: Vibrators do not need to be shaped like penises.*
3. *Something in your arse, withdrawn shortly before a clitoral orgasm can feel AMAZING for some people.*
4. *Lube is great. Don't worry about the sheets; you can wash them. Never run out of lube. Especially if you're doing anything with your arse.*

Who ever said that lesbians can't have sex? We beg to differ.

Role-Play

Like gay men, some women prefer to role-play the more dominant or "top" role, while others prefer to be a "bottom"—a less active role.

HOWEVER, I think it's worth noting that the idea of roles is far from unique to men and women of a gay or bi persuasion. Many straight couples will experiment with power play as well, with one partner being more submissive to the other. Gay people did not invent this concept. Just look at that whole *Fifty Shades* malarkey.

For some gay people, the idea of "top or bottom" or "active or passive" is an important part of being sexually fulfilled.

> [Roles] shouldn't matter; however people are wired different ways. Some people regard certain sexual acts as either preferences or necessities. If someone can only be aroused by being dominated, then it's good that they're open about that in order to find someone who will fulfill that need.
>
> —Stuart, 33, UK

> They [roles] did matter for a while. I spent a few years experimenting with sub/dom. I had a partner who was

strictly dom and would play games both in the bedroom and in public. Like, we would be in a restaurant and I would only be allowed to eat my lunch with my left hand, for example, unless she told me otherwise. Or a few times we went to Klub Fuk and she'd flog me in front of everyone or whatever. That's all fun for a while, but I'm a bit older now and it's started to feel a bit silly or boring recently.

—Fi, 29, Madrid, Spain

If it's for a quick shag on Grindr, etc., then yes [roles matter]. I don't use those sort of apps to have a chat or make friends. It's always better to be having sex with someone compatible with you in that regard though. Wanking is something I do on my own, so not really up for just doing that with a partner.

—Jonny, London, UK

TRANS SEX

The sex lives of trans people can be a little more complicated than most, but they need not be. **There is one important thing to remember—people don't fall in love with genitalia.**

As most transsexuals living in their preferred gender are

upfront about this, either when meeting people or online, their partners enter into relationships knowing full well what private parts their new paramour possesses; therefore, it's not an issue. Some people actively seek trans partners— both pre- and post-op.

Some trans people can opt for genital surgery, while others prefer not to, so this will obviously affect a person's sex life.

The same smorgasbord of sexual activities is available to trans people as to gay or straight people. Any hole's a goal (just kidding!) and everywhere feels nice.

> Sex between women is very different than heterosexual sex. There's no prearranged goal of ejaculation and orgasm. So I think dating women, as a woman, is in that sense easier—the sex is a little more casual. Where does the line between kissing or even talking and sex begin? We in the kink community are aware that there are a multitude of ways people can "have sex" and achieve gratification without touching and without orgasm. So this is all very fuzzy.
>
> However, I think that applies to the *lesbian* experience more than to the transgender woman experience. Your mileage may vary.
>
> There's also the fetishization of (particularly) trans

women. If you look at the personals on Craigslist, you will see various sections, w4m, m4w, w4w, and so on. But there's also t4m and m4t. The problem with this is that there are men out there who I assume are curious about sex with men and so seek out women (which feels safe and normal to them) who have penises (which indulges their curiosity about sex with men). But I am not a man. And my sexual "response profile" is very different than a man. That tissue that men are familiar with, it doesn't work the same on a trans woman. My emotional response is different. So these personals and dating sites particularly for "trans" people (to include cross-dressers and drag queens, the post-op, pre-op, and non-op trans people, etc., etc.), are almost entirely about fetishization. Which I don't want. I want to be treated as a woman.

—Jane, Washington

But, seriously, whoever you are, whatever gender you identify with, and however many labels you wear, there are two rules to good sex:

1. Do what feels nice.
2. Communicate with your partner. (How else are you going to find out what feels nice for him or her, and how would they know what feels nice for you?)

WHY ARE GAY MEN SO SLUTTY?

Well, first of all, I don't like the word slutty, so let's rephrase that to it's proper word, PROMISCUOUS, which basically means "has sex with multiple partners." Second of all, anyone who suggests that all gay men are promiscuous is a raging homophobe.

HOWEVER, the fact of the matter is that many stereotypes have a seed of truth lurking under all the horse crap. In this instance, both my own research and that of other writers suggests that gay men do seem inclined to promiscuity. In my survey, ONLY gay men reported having more than twenty partners in their lifetime, with several reporting they had had sex with more than a hundred.

This is not meant to be shocking. It is simply a fact. Remember, as young gay people, we were raised on HETERONORMATIVE VALUES, which means the values of the straight people who are in the majority.

Until very, very recently, same-sex couples couldn't even get married, so OF COURSE LGBTQ+ people haven't always played by the same rules as our heterosexual brothers and sisters. The gay scene has its own norms, and one of those norms, it seems, is promiscuity.

Some theories about gay male promiscuity:

1. **BOYS WILL BE BOYS:** We (and that's all of us,

women too) get RAGINGLY HORNY because of TESTOSTERONE—a hormone. Men make more of it than women. Fact. From an evolutionary perspective, a male could make about fifty babies in the time it takes a female to have one. It is thought that monogamy (having one sexual partner) stems from our prehistoric need to have a male hunter-gatherer handy to help provide for a female's offspring. Basically, the only reason straight men aren't having as much sex as gay ones is because their girlfriends would have them out on the street in a heartbeat.

This theory is somewhat supported by research that suggests men are more likely to cheat than women.

Well, imagine women are removed from the equation—like-minded gay men can have all the sex they like, without the risk of falling pregnant.

This does not excuse bad behavior. As higher mammals, we have evolved beyond simply reacting to the chemicals in our bodies and we are not ruled by them. No man, gay or straight, HAS to be promiscuous or a shady cheater.

2. **NORMALIZED BEHAVIORS:** Promiscuity is perhaps most associated with the larger "gay

scenes"—cities and towns where a lot of gay men tend to live. Within gay subcultures, men are supportive and nonjudgmental of promiscuity; therefore, it becomes a social norm. Again, this does not excuse bad behavior such as cheating on a partner or having lots and lots of unsafe sex.

3. **MISOGYNY:** Years of sexist dung has embedded the idea that promiscuous men are legends and promiscuous women should be dragged through the village square tied to the back of cart dressed as Moll Flanders (look it up). Men, gay or straight, are not subjected to the same shaming as women, although I would argue that this is changing—everyone sees sleeping around as a little tacky, even gay men who are doing so, paradoxically.

I also wonder why, if straight men look like dogs if they treat women badly, gay men are seen (wrongly) as "tough" and can treat each other as badly as they like. Women tend to frown on promiscuous straight men, but are often nonjudgmental of promiscuous gay ones.

American therapist Alan Downs talks a lot about promiscuity in his book *The Velvet Rage*, which you could read if you're interested in this sort of thing. He writes only about gay men but believes (some) gay men behave the way they do because of an internalized homophobia that he calls "shame."

Feeling we're weird and wrong (which goes back to the "different" and "not normal" labels) has, he says, led us to believe we are unlovable, so we act that out in various ways, one of which is casual sex with multiple partners. He believes we are seeking external validation through physical acceptance by sexual partners. Doctors and nurses in sexual health clinics would probably agree that SOME gay men's attitudes toward sex are unhealthy. For whatever reason, gay men are more predisposed to addiction problems, including sex addiction, but that is not ALL gay men.

I am less sure than Alan Downs. There is nothing wrong with having multiple sexual partners. GASP—BURN THE HERETIC! I know, right? If all partners are **honest, open, and safe** about their lifestyle choices, it makes no difference how many sexual partners you have—but don't go picking on someone else's patch, mind! No one likes a boyfriend or girlfriend stealer!

It's about CHOICES, and I believe everyone should be able to live the way they want to live as long as they *don't hurt anyone else* OR THEMSELVES in the process. You can choose to be promiscuous or you can choose not to be.

Regardless of how many partners your friends have, regardless of how horny you are, regardless of how many offers you get...the CHOICE is always yours.

YOU MUST ALWAYS PRACTICE SAFE SEX

And now for the bad news. **The more sexual partners you have, the more likely you are to pick up an STI, a sexually transmitted infection.** There are numerous ones out there, some worse than others; most are treatable and all are avoidable.

A little slice of good news: Statistically, gay women are at a low risk of STIs as long as they make sure any toys are cleaned (and you can put condoms on them too).

Infections that can be transmitted by blood, however, can be passed, in theory, through bleeding gums or cuts on fingers. **No one is ever risk free** (something to think about before you cheat on a partner).

More bad news: Statistically speaking, gay men are in a high-risk category. This is mainly down to promiscuity on the gay scene. Hey! Don't shoot the messenger! Again, the more partners you have, the more likely you are to get an STI.

Get ready to feel some high-intensity psychosomatic itching! Let's take a look at some common STIs:

1. **Genital herpes:** Nasty, painful, and itchy sores on your penis, vagina, mouth, or anus. Basically, a cold sore on the knob or fee-fee. Cannot be cured (you'll carry a dormant version of the virus for life) but can be treated. Once infected, victims may well experience further itchy/painful episodes.

2. **Gonorrhea:** Although this infection is not always symptomatic, the most pressing symptom is a burning sensation when you pee. Some sufferers may also get a delightful puslike discharge from the penis or vagina. As the infection is bacterial, it can be treated with antibiotics, although doctors are becoming increasingly worried about this infection's resistance to treatment.

3. **Genital warts:** Genital warts are caused by a virus called HPV, which is present in about thirty percent of all sexually active people. It's highly

contagious but, of the people who have it, only about three percent will ever develop a wart on the penis, vagina, or anus. Visible warts can be treated with wart-removal cream, cryotherapy (freezing them off), excision (cutting them off—ouch!), or electro- or laser therapy (to burn them off). As if those methods weren't pleasant enough, the virus remains forever and recurrence is possible.

4. **Syphilis:** Large, non-itchy, non-painful ulcers on the genitals or anus are the first sign of syphilis. This one needs to be treated quickly with antibiotics or there could be secondary symptoms. If left untreated, it can affect the brain, eventually leading to death. Cheery.

5. **Crabs:** This one is confusing. WHY would you have crabs down there? Turns out "crabs" is a name for "pubic lice"—sort of nits for your pubes. You can see them AND they're super itchy. They can be treated with a lotion, but they can be a bugger to get rid of. As well as the itching, crabs have the embarrassing side effect of your having to confess to your parents, because the lice can live on bedding, clothes, and towels. Therefore, affected items need to be boil washed before you potentially give your mom crabs.

6. **Chlamydia:** In about fifty percent of cases, you

might experience a slight discharge or a burning sensation when you pee. Or you might have chlamydia and never know it because you don't have any symptoms. The consequences for women are much more serious, as the bacteria can lead to severe reproductive problems. (It's worth noting that chlamydia can lead to sterility in men too). In 2019, a total of 1,808,703 chlamydial infections were reported to the Center for Disease Control (CDC). That's just the ones who were treated too.

7. **Hepatitis B and C:** There's a whole alphabet of hepatitis viruses out there, but these are the ones mostly commonly transmitted via sex. They are infections of the liver and can be very serious. Hepatitis B can be vaccinated against (there is as yet no vaccine for hepatitis C).

HIV/AIDS

This one gets its own special section because it's of particular importance to gay and bi men, who (in the Western world) are the **highest-risk** group for this infection. Women, do be aware that HIV can be transmitted via oral sex, but you are not in a high-risk group, statistically speaking.

For my generation, being gay and dying of AIDS were

cruelly linked. Young gay guys in the eighties and nineties feared coming out for this very reason, like we said earlier.

New cases of HIV are increasing in young gay and bi men. How can this be, when we ALL know to use condoms, especially for anal sex? Two reasons: First, the campaign warning people about HIV and AIDS terrified a generation. As the nineties progressed, people better understood prevention and medication and HIV/AIDS seemed to slip out of the media and collective conscious. This means that education about HIV is poorer than it used to be. The second reason is that triumphant breakthroughs in the treatment of HIV mean that people live with the virus for much, much longer (which is great, obviously—no one likes dying) and are therefore infectious for longer, coming into contact with more sexual partners.

This means we need to change how we view HIV (relatively few people go on to develop AIDS anymore if treated).

What Is HIV?

HIV (human immunodeficiency virus) is a hardcore virus that attacks a host's immune system, making it very hard for the body to defend itself from illness. AIDS (acquired immune deficiency syndrome) CANNOT be "caught" but refers to the illnesses a person with HIV might develop as a result of their condition.

How Do You Get HIV?

You can get HIV by coming into contact with the blood or semen of someone else who is already HIV positive. By far the most common way to do this is through unprotected (no condom) anal sex.

Can You Get HIV through Oral Sex?

Yes, although the risk is much, much less than with anal sex. It is possible because people can suffer bleeding gums, making the recipient vulnerable to the virus through his partner's cum or pre-cum. Catching HIV through oral sex is very, very rare. But it can happen, so be aware!

Is There a Cure for HIV?

There is no cure for HIV. Many HIV-positive people are under treatment to keep them as healthy as possible.

How Common Is HIV?

Around 1.2 million people in the U.S. are HIV positive, but—and here comes the scary bit—14 percent of these people DON'T KNOW IT because they are not being tested regularly.

According to HIV.gov, an estimated 36,400 new HIV infections occurred in the United States in 2018.

From 2014 to 2018, the number of diagnoses of HIV

infection for transgender male-to-female (MTF) and transgender female-to-male (FTM) adults and adolescents increased.

What Is Viral Load?

The term "viral load" refers to how much HIV is in a person's blood at a given time. With the right treatment, most sufferers can get their load down to an "undetectable" level, which means they are far, far less likely to pass the virus on to a sexual partner.

A person's viral load is at its highest immediately after infection and before treatment is started. This is when a person is most infectious.

What Is PEP?

PEP stands for **post-exposure prophylaxis**. If a person is exposed to HIV, they can be treated with PEP for up to seventy-two (but preferably within twenty-four) hours after exposure.

PEP is NOT a substitute for a condom and can have very unpleasant side effects. However, if taken correctly over a monthlong period, PEP can stop HIV infection. It can be obtained in emergency rooms or sexual health clinics, where they will assess your level of risk (see "Helpful Numbers and Websites and Stuff" at the back of the book).

What Is PrEP?

Now, people in "high-risk" groups—including gay and bi men, trans women, and sex workers—can access PrEP (PRE-exposure prophylaxis). This is a cautionary dose of PEP that means a person is highly unlikely to become infected with HIV in the first place if it's taken correctly.

After lengthy trials, PrEP is now available in all parts of the United States through your doctor or health care provider.

It's important to know that PrEP *doesn't* protect you from other sexually transmitted diseases or unwanted pregnancy, so it's still important to use condoms and have regular sexual health tests. If you aren't taking PrEP, you must wear a condom.

What Can I Do?

HIV is everyone's business. HIV doesn't discriminate between old and young, black or white, top or bottom, gay or straight. We all tend to think "it won't happen to me"... until it does.

You might think that's simplistic, but it's also true. The best way to ensure you don't get HIV is to always wear a condom when you have anal sex. (This also goes for all the other fun STIs I mentioned.) I can sense eye rolling...

"Porn stars never wear condoms"—Yup, but they get tested every month. Even then, a recent HIV outbreak shut down the porn industry after a number of actors became infected.

"It's sexier without a condom"—Okay, but you might get HIV. Which is not sexy.

"He says he's HIV negative"—He can't be sure. Even if he had an HIV test that day, that is only an indication of his HIV status **six weeks ago**, as that is how long it takes the virus to show up in the blood.

As well as always wearing a condom, **it's a good idea to have an HIV test about every six months** if you are sexually active.

Why? As I said above, you are at your most infectious in the early days. Knowing early means it's less likely you could pass on the virus, and you can get on treatment faster, which is better for you too.

Your health is your responsibility.

KRISTIAN'S STORY

Every morning, I wake up, and the first thing I do after throwing the alarm clock across the room is go to the bathroom, where I carefully place two bits of plastic onto my eyeballs so I can see properly.

Yes, I'm short-sighted. Shocking, isn't it? I mean, you wouldn't know unless I told you. But yep, I genuinely can't see my hand in front of my face without my lenses.

Being short-sighted isn't my fault; it's just something that happened to me.

And an hour later, before I leave the house for work, I tip four small tablets into my hand and knock them back with a glass of milk, to help my immune system cope with the effects of the HIV virus.

So there's two things you wouldn't guess from just looking at me.

Despite what you may have heard, HIV is no longer the killer it used to be. Sorry to disappoint anyone wondering if I look like Tom Hanks did at the end of *Philadelphia*, but I'm actually quite normal looking. Some might even say buff—although my fondness for cookies tends to put paid to anything resembling the six pack I had in my early twenties. Being HIV positive isn't "dramatic" on a daily basis. But then again I've had about twelve years to get used to the idea. I'm not going to bore you with the details of how I got it. Had sex, didn't think about the consequences. Thought I was invincible. Wasn't. Was I a slag? No. Was I an idiot? Categorically yes. I remember getting diagnosed, back when I was twenty-two. I wish I could say I felt angry, shocked, stunned, wretched, hysterical, whatever. I didn't. I just felt like a cliché. Another goddamn statistic. And for what? Half an hour of giddy bareback sex? Sitting there in the clinic. It just felt so...pointless.

Fast-forward twelve years and life is pretty calm and mundane. I mean, right now, the biggest stresses in my life are managing my chronic insomnia and finding a route to work that doesn't involve sitting in my car for an hour and a half on the M25. Let me just make one thing clear, however: HIV is NOT a walk in the park. It's difficult at times. I've been in a monogamous relationship for the past three years with an HIV-negative man. It required a fair bit of soul searching on my part before I actually bit the bullet and made a commitment to him. You see, when you love someone, you want to protect them, and exposing them to a lifelong virus for the sake of getting your end away requires a strong mind and an even stronger relationship. We cope. Our condom bill is huge.

Modern medication is excellent. I suffer a little with side effects, insomnia being one of them (see above), and diarrhea being another, but it's something I've learned to live with. Like having a limp. As a single guy I was always upfront with guys. I figured if they had a problem with me being HIV positive, it said a hell of a lot more about them than it did about me. I read profiles on dating sites saying "Clean only" and "HIV negative—you should be too" and all I saw was fear and ignorance. You see, having sex with a positive guy isn't a death sentence. Actually, if he tells you he's positive, it's far more likely that he's health aware, on meds, and therefore has undetectable levels of the virus in his system. To put it bluntly: He's pretty uninfectious. And when you take into account that over a quarter of people with HIV don't know they've got it [in the UK], it's easy to do the math. No medication means uncontrollable amounts of HIV and a pretty infectious sexual partner.

If you ask my boyfriend, he'd rather be in a relationship with someone like me who's got his HIV under control, than to rock out of a club every Saturday with some random who might not know or might not care. As I've said to many naysayers on Gaydar and Grindr in my single years—"I'm not the first person you've ever slept with who's got HIV; I'm just the first who's been nice enough to tell you."

Would I go back and do things differently given the chance? Maybe. I wish I could get rid of the virus and keep everything I've learned from it. You see, it's kind of made me the person I am today, and that bloke isn't half-bad. Living with HIV has taught me responsibility. It's taught me compassion. It's made me a lot less selfish.

At the age of twenty-two or twenty-three—whenever it was—I was wasting my life. I was checking out of reality in a haze of booze, drugs, clubs, and sex. When the doctor spoke the words "Kristian, I'm afraid your test has come back positive," my world changed forever.

Living with HIV has made me grow up. After I'd processed the emotional fallout, I realized I wasn't going to die. Moreover, I realized I wanted to live.

I wanted to help others like me. And all of a sudden my life had a purpose. Sounds schmaltzy? Develop a lifelong condition and see if it doesn't give you an epiphany.

Nowadays I have a career, a relationship, and a future. I do a lot of work in driving down stigma and raising awareness of HIV-related issues. These days I'm proud to look people in the eye and tell them who I am and what

HIV has made me. I get satisfaction from helping the newly diagnosed or those who are struggling. I feel pride when I look at what I've achieved. A straight male friend of mine texted me the other day to say he was taking part in human vaccine trials. He did it because my story had opened his eyes. I'm proud of that. I'm proud to have inspired people.

HIV isn't a death sentence. Like I said, my life is pretty normal and—barring any wayward out-of-control buses—I reckon I'll live a relatively long life. I won't lie and say that HIV is a barrel of laughs to deal with, but in many ways, it's actually made my life a lot richer. I really hope that one day we can find a cure. But in the meantime, I'd really love to find that quicker route into work...

THE BEST WAY TO PROTECT YOURSELF AGAINST ALL STIs IS TO WEAR A CONDOM EVERY TIME YOU HAVE SEX.

For oral sex, some people use condoms or dental dams too.

SAUNAS AND SEX PARTIES

As this is a guide to ALL things gay, it would be wrong of me not to mention the things most brochures would gloss over.

In big cities all around the world, there are places that cater to gay men's seeming obsession with sex.

Saunas, or "bath houses," are dotted all over the country, and they are perfectly legal. People (many saunas run lesbian nights) pay some money to enter and then have a bit of a sauna and some random sex.

Again, this is fine as long as you're **safe**.

That said, NEVER ONCE did I hear ANYONE say, "This is my husband, Derek. We met at Chariots in Vauxhall and it was TRUE LOVE." Saunas are regarded as a little sleazy, and people often visit these places in secret. It is also true that sexual health clinics often have to treat people who have been to saunas and come away with a little more than healthy, glowing skin...

The advent of the sex app has also removed the need to pay an entry fee. In big cities, people often use the apps to invite a load of people round for a "party" or a "chill out." These are code words for an orgy, simple as that. Very often, there are drugs involved (which is silly because nothing makes a cock go floppy like many drugs—therefore, guys also have to take a load of Viagra. How EXHAUSTING). SOME sources suggest such parties are partly to blame for the sharp rise in HIV, syphilis, and hepatitis on the gay scene. Jeez, remember when "parties" were about ice cream and hot dogs? Sigh. Let's go back to that.

CLEARLY, going to some random's apartment with a load of guys you don't know is a bit on the safety dubious side. And, dear God, wear a condom.

SEX AND LOVE

Homosexual people love a lot of sex, but we also love a lot of love. Every day, all over the world, you'll find gay men and women deeply, TOTALLY in love, and they have something better than just sex. They have intimacy, warmth, passion, and LOVE—the NEED to be with their partner. Also:

sex ≠ love

You can have all the sex in the world, but it (quite literally) isn't filling the same hole. I believe we all want to be loved.

This chapter was all about sex, not intimacy. You can't find instant intimacy in a dark room or on Grindr. More valuable than bum or muff fun is holding hands, kisses, and hugs. I'm sure some of you are miming sticking two fingers down your throat, but IT'S TRUE. Lots of LGBTQ+ people don't even have sex but can totally identify as gay, bi, or straight because of who they seek intimacy with and who they LOVE. By all means, enjoy sex, but if you go looking for sex because you're hungry for love, you'll starve.

CHAPTER 10
NESTING

Q: What does a lesbian bring on a second date?

A: A moving van.

It's one of the oldest stereotypes in the gay book (literally in this case, which is quite meta if you think about it). Perhaps without men to make a mess of things, women are just far better at commitment. In any case, stereotypically, gay women are thought to jump to the cozy cohabitation phase at record speeds.

Of course, this, like any stereotype, has an iota of truth. All kidding aside, many LGBTQ+ women **and** men do choose monogamous, committed relationships. This might be something you would like to happen now or further down the line but, however you identify, you have lots of choices about your future.

This decision actually opens a can of worms about norms, nature, and nurture. Some questions to consider:

- **Why do we seek commitment?**
- **How do you make love last?**
- **Do gay couples emulate straight norms?**
- **Are we biologically programmed toward monogamy or promiscuity?**

WHY BOTHER?

Even though very few mammals in the natural world form committed, monogamous pairings, humans do seem programmed toward it. Even the hardiest singles seem to settle down in the end. There are a multitude of benefits to being in a relationship:

- **Love**—Sometimes the thought of being without someone is just too awful to stand. Being in love is like having a best friend supersized. Just make sure one person doesn't become your whole world—that's never, ever healthy.

- **Companionship**—Life is long and lonely if you do everything alone. Independence is vital, but so is company. Sooner or later, your friends may well settle down, and where will that leave you?

- **Comfort**—Yeah, going out on the prowl is awesome, but so are cozy walks in the park and reading the papers in bed on a Sunday morning.

- **Sex**—Finding new sexual partners is a thrill, but having one partner who knows what they're doing tops that. Also, monogamy is much less risky health-wise, obviously.

- **Security**—Some people just feel happier and calmer knowing there's someone special in their life, someone who knows your Starbucks order without having to ask.

- **Financial**—If we're being cold about it, the system is set up to benefit couples of all orientations. Combining incomes always makes practical sense.

However, all these things combined don't mean anything if you're with the wrong person.

NOT BEING IN A RELATIONSHIP IS BETTER THAN BEING IN THE WRONG RELATIONSHIP.

Always.

I'm afraid it's not all hugs and snuggles. Same-sex relationships are open to all the same pitfalls as straight ones—cheating, lying, jealousy, abuse, emotional blackmail, bickering, controlling behavior. What has always surprised me is how people will tolerate these things purely because they are scared of being alone or can't be bothered with the hassle of gays bars and Grindr.

News just in: those aren't the only two options.

We've already talked about how you can meet people and where to go on dates, but how do you convert dating into something more long term? We're talking THE LOCKDOWN.

This is the point at which you change your Facebook status, tell your mom, delete Grindr, etc. We're talking about having a PROPER girlfriend or boyfriend.

The lockdown is a critical point in a new relationship—I call it the "poo-or-get-off-the-pot" moment. Basically, you have to decide if the person you're with is worth giving up the potential Malik/Grande waiting just around the corner. How do you know?

Well, this is why you date. People who try to rush you into lockdown need to CTFO. If you're taking yourself off the market, then, as with house buying, you need to carry out the full architectural survey before purchase.

Especially on the gay scene, surrounded by a constant stream of pecs, dicks, tits, and vaginas, it's hard to settle for just one, but remember—if the person you're with is kind, funny, loyal, giving, and loving, then these are things you won't find in a pair of big arms off Grindr or a cute ass at a bar.

PROMISCUITY VS. MONOGAMY

Both positions have pros and cons:

Monogamy Pros	Monogamy Cons
Intimacy	Lack of variety
Comfort	Missing out
Promiscuity Pros	**Promiscuity Cons**
Variety	Loneliness
Freedom	Sitting at the freak table at weddings

Of course, some couples have decided to have their cake and indeed eat it. We're talking **open relationships**. A 2010 study of six hundred gay male couples found that about fifty percent were in an open relationship, so it's not uncommon on the gay scene.

An open relationship is one with a cat flap allowing other people to drift in and out of the bedroom. Sometimes this might mean threesomes (or moresomes) with other people, or both partners being able to play away from home. All the intimacy with your partner, all the variety with extras.

Perfect, right? Cakealicious! Marie Antoinette would approve. (FYI, a lot of people think Ms. Antoinette was #TeamBi.) You might question why everyone isn't doing this.

There is a very strong argument to suggest that monogamy is a societal or religious construct—remember how

I said most mammals DON'T mate for life, and you can pretty much track the rise of monogamy around the globe with Christian missionaries (the same route, by the way, they took to tell people that same-sex activity was wrong).

It's thought that monogamy is the best way to provide a stable home for children, although this is a horribly outdated perspective in a country with a divorce rate like ours.

So why is ANYONE monogamous?

For one thing, it's the IDEAL. We didn't grow up hearing about the bit after the wedding where Prince Charming tells Cinderella he wants to be able to see other people. Certainly for gay couples with families, you can see why a degree of stability is best. Finally, as I've said before, I don't think it's ever entirely possible to keep emotions out of the boudoir...

At least part of the reason seems to relate to control. It's simply a bit ICKY to think of your beloved poking his or her private parts in someone else's face. The mere thought is enough to put most couples off:

> [My boyfriend and I ruled out sex with other people] because our relationship was too unstable and new. We were both getting jealous and suspicious over nothing. Neither of us like the idea of the other doing things [with other men], even though we both felt we should.
>
> —N, 27, Sydney, Australia

> I've thought about [having an open relationship] a lot
> and like the idea in theory, but the fact is it wouldn't be
> totally safe, and I hate the idea of exposing my boyfriend
> to STIs. Of course I see other guys and fancy them,
> but you just have to accept that you made a choice to
> commit to one guy.
>
> —Ben, 23, Manchester, UK

> There's no way I'd have an open relationship. I've been
> with my partner for eight years, and we have ups and
> downs, but I love her and don't want to have sex with
> anyone else.
>
> —Jenny, 31, Dublin, Ireland

For some, cheating is cheating and that is that. Jealousy and paranoia are enough to make a peen shrivel like a salted slug or a vag slam shut like a clam—NOT SEXY. For most, having sex with other people is a deal breaker and you may have to respect that or find a more compatible partner.

However, all people—gay or otherwise—must recognize that there is **one universal truth of the universe:**

WE ALL WANT TO HAVE SEX WITH LOADS OF PEOPLE. (UNLESS YOU'RE ASEXUAL, OBVS.)

Allow me to explain. We don't ALL want to cheat on our partners or be promiscuous, but—and please correct me if I'm wrong (although I know you're lying)—when we see someone we fancy, we can't help but fancy them! Short of scooping out our eyes with melon ballers, there's little we can do about this.

So it becomes a question of impulse control. If we all accept it's perfectly natural to have urges, we are, I'm sure, sufficiently evolved not to have to act on them.

For some couples, though, the idea of having to suppress urges is crazy, and so they allow each other the freedom to act on their desires.

In most open relationships, there are certain RULES. These often include:

- Safe sex only (well, duh).
- No anal (in the case of gay and bi men).
- Never in the home.
- Never on each other's time.
- No last names.
- No kissing.
- No repeat performances (only one-off hookups).

Although, with so many rules, one does have to question how much "freedom" couples really have.

JAY'S STORY

My partner and I have been together for eight years. We're civil partners, living together in our own place—in short we're quite "settled" with each other. We're best friends as well as partners and know each other inside out.

A few years ago, we agreed that we could see other people, should the opportunity arise. It wasn't something that was decided for us to instantly run out and flirt with the first man we met—it was more "If the moment happens, then its not a problem." There are rules: We're not allowed to bring anyone back to our own home (unless we're together); you don't wake up at someone else's place; and we always tell the other person when something happens.

As for why we chose to do it, the first is down to the obvious: something new. As well as obviously being a lot of fun, sex can also be a learning experience and therapeutic—and one way which this is demonstrated at its best is in its variety. We realized that while we're still committed to each other and have total faith in one another, seeing other people not only enriched our sex lives but made us stronger as a couple. A further reason is that now, with hindsight and still in my twenties, committing yourself to one person for sex almost feels abnormal, particularly for gay couples, where (in most cases) the prospect of raising children and settling down in the traditional sense is nonexistent. (My partner and I are strongly against the idea of having children. Ever.)

YOUNG LOVE

Lots of younger LGBTQ+ people want to be in committed relationships—after all, that intimacy does look good, doesn't it? Well, it does, but remember, having no relationship is better than having one just because everyone else is. Would you jump off a cliff if your friends told you to? (ANSWER: How high is this cliff we're talkin' about?)

When I visit schools, most now have at least one "gay couple" and, importantly, the rest of the school doesn't seem to give a flying fig. Schools are legally required to provide a safe space for all pupils so, IN THEORY, you should be able to have a relationship with a classmate. In practice, schools vary widely, with some far better than others at tackling homophobic bullying.

Outside of school, there's nothing to stop you having a

boyfriend or girlfriend at all. Some couples I know in their thirties got together when they were at school and are going strong to this day!

This said, few people wind up with their childhood sweethearts, and not everyone is emotionally mature enough to have a relationship while still at school or college. Early boyfriends or girlfriends, however, are FAB because it gives you a taste of what being in a relationship is like, teaches you how to compromise, and allows you to establish what you like and don't like.

"GAY MARRIAGE"

It's a really exciting time to be LGBTQ+ in America. In 2015 the U.S. Supreme Court made same-sex marriages legal in all fifty states in *Obergefell v. Hodges*.

Same-sex marriage has been legal all over Canada since 2005. The UK has now also fully legalized gay marriage. Rejoice! Whether you want to get married or not, I believe that everyone should be entitled to exactly the same institutions. The LGBTQ+ community is divided on this subject, however—and with said institutions being historically pissy with us, who can blame them.

I am strongly in favor [of same-sex marriage]. I believe the halfway house of civil partnerships was merely a stepping stone in enabling full equality for the LBGT community. Love is the same regardless of sexuality, and marriage does not belong to anyone, religious or otherwise—it is a human social construct, and it should be open to all couples who wish to commit to each other. Yes, if the right man were to ask me, I would love to have a husband!

—Mike, London, UK

I see no difference at all between gay and straight marriage, and I can't believe in the twenty-first century people still distinguish between the two. Marriage is marriage; love is love.

—MJ, UK

I'm very much in support of equal rights for LGBTQ+
people, including marital rights. Same-sex marriage
has been legal in my country, South Africa, for seven
years, and society has yet to crumble. I quite like the
idea of getting married one day—mostly because I love
weddings, if I'm honest.

—Stephen, 22, Johannesburg, South Africa

I absolutely support same-sex marriage. And I find any
argument against it absolutely ridiculous. This may sound
harsh, but there is one simple reason: Whether or not two
people of the same sex can get married has absolutely no
impact on the lives or marriages of anybody else. Literally
not the tiniest impact. And that's all there is to it. It's nobody
else's business, so there is no sense in opposing it.

Personally, I don't really want to get married, but it
is important for me to know that, if I change my mind, I
have the possibility to.

—Anna, 17, Germany

I actually don't feel very strongly about this. For me, it's
solely a legal/practical thing. All the fuss and sentimentality
is meaningless to me when you can just get a divorce
and void the whole thing if you change your mind.

—L, 28, Brighton, UK

GAYBIES

Hopefully it won't come as too much of a surprise when I tell you two men or two women will need a little help when it comes to making a baby happen. WHAAAAAT? I know, it's true. You need a healthy supply of both egg and sperm, I'm afraid.

That said, this is but a tiny barrier in stopping same-sex couples from starting a family, and many are choosing to do so. Again, this is a matter of EQUALITY—just because we fancy who we fancy, it doesn't mean we shouldn't be granted the same choices as the majority.

As with marriage, this is a contentious issue (who knows why, it's the twenty-first century).

> I'd dearly love to be a father one day. Being a single gay man, though, I don't know quite how that will happen.
> —Stuart, 33, Brighton, UK

> I think people who think through the idea of children and then make a conscious decision to have them are always better parents than those who just have them because "that's what you do."
> —Fi, 29, Madrid, Spain

I think good parents are needed everywhere; their persuasion is irrelevant other than giving a good life to a child. I would love to adopt a child when I have a secure relationship and financial situation. I would prefer to adopt than have my own. I don't like the idea of being pregnant, but I do feel maternal, and I know there are so many children out there who need loving homes.

—Blaz, 34, Bristol, UK

None of the arguments against gay parenting make much sense to me because they basically seem to fall into two categories: 1. "Children need a mother and a father because they bring different things to the family"—this makes as much sense to me as saying, "Children need one musical parent and one scientific parent" or, "Children need one humorous parent and one very serious parent." Obviously, different people will bring different things to a child's upbringing, but insisting it must be one man and one woman seems random. The "nature" argument never stands up that well either. "Children will be bullied if they have gay parents"—kids can be bullied for any number of things, and that's not really a basis to say those things shouldn't happen. In time, having gay parents will be as unremarkable as having divorced parents.

—L, 28, Brighton, UK

L makes a very good point. The arguments against same-sex couples having children are wafer thin. There is basically NO REASON ON EARTH that we shouldn't have families. "Oh, but they'll get picked on!" scream homophobic readers clutching their pearls. "Only by you, you small-minded twonks," replies the rest of the world.

Two loving parents = two GREAT parents, regardless of sexual preference or gender identity. Got that? Good.

HOW TO MAKE A BABY HAPPEN THE GAY WAY

1. **Sperm donation:** A female couple can use donor sperm to become preggo. The NHS recommends you acquire love juice via a registered clinic, as it will have been screened for STIs and genetic abnormalities. What's more, if you go through a registered clinic, both mothers will automatically be recorded as the baby's parents. If you aren't married and use a private donor, the mother who doesn't give birth to the infant will have to later adopt it.

I have always wanted to have a family, and I never felt that being gay would prevent that. I met my partner nine years ago, and after our civil partnership in 2009, we started to talk about creating a family. We both knew that we wanted to have children, but had not settled on the best way to do it. As a lesbian, there are so many options. We considered all of them—known donor, unknown donor, adoption, etc. We discussed each option together, we met with a family planner, and we talked with friends. And finally, we arrived at a way forward that felt comfortable for us. My partner would have the babies through an unknown but open donor that we selected from a clinic in New York. Now, we have a beautiful eighteen-month-old daughter and we couldn't be happier. We both work four days per week, and both do child care one day a week. We appreciate the equality in our relationship and that both of us are able to feel fulfilled professionally and personally, as mothers.

—Charlotte, London, UK

2. **Co-parenting:** This is traditionally where a gay man and woman team up and raise a child together—perhaps sharing custody between gay couples. It's not always two gay parents; one can clearly be straight. However, as anyone who has seen the shiteous Madonna film *Next Best Thing* will know, make sure you have a lawyer handy to ensure that the arrangement is legally binding.

3. **Surrogacy:** Sometimes gay men (or women who do not wish to be preggers) will enlist a surrogate to carry an egg they have fertilized. Surrogacy laws vary from state to state. SOME U.S. jurisdictions allow surrogates to commercially advertise, while others don't. There is still a risk that a surrogate baby won't be handed over, which means the process is fraught with uncertainty.

4. **Adoption:** Adoption laws vary from state to state, but most now support LGBTQ+ couples or individuals adopting, and local authorities and agencies are crying out for new parents. The challenge with adoption is that many children needing adoptive parents have traumatic backgrounds and will often need extra love, support, and stability.

So as you can see, becoming same-sex parents is

something you have to really want to do. To me, it hardly seems fair that straight people only need neglect a condom and BOOM, they get a family. Alas, them's the breaks.

Parenting, should you want to embark down that road, is the most amazing gift a human can give.

MATHEW'S STORY

Mathew and his partner started a family in South Africa but have lived in London for the past few years.

> We were not unusual in our position of wanting to have a family—I think that this is a desire most people have to some extent or another. Our challenge was that the only way this could be achieved was through pursuing the surrogacy route. We knew it would be challenging and costly, both financially and emotionally. But our desire for a family was strong and this pushed us along.
>
> Having children with a surrogate mother broadly falls into two categories—either using the eggs of the surrogate mother or using an egg donor. The decision to pursue either route has a number of pros and cons, and in the end we chose the latter approach—that of sourcing a separate egg donor. We set out to find three key people to assist us in our journey. We needed a social

worker to help us with all of the legal requirements, an egg donor, and a surrogate mother. Additionally, we needed a facility to help with all of the necessary laboratory requirements. With the help of friends and acquaintances, we managed to find a surrogate mother who was available and met our requirements. Additionally, we made contact with a helpful and encouraging social worker, and through the fertility clinic and the wonderful assistance of our appointed nurse, an egg donor was sourced, as well as a facility to get our surrogate pregnant.

Once all of these people were in place, we met with a specialized lawyer who helped us draw up a contract with the surrogate mother and all that this entailed. The current legal situation is a little different from what it was when we did our contract, but there were certain requirements that we had to meet, including undergoing medicals, financial assessments, etc., for the adoption process that would have to be followed once the baby or babies were born.

With everything in place, the clinic soon organized the donor and surrogate and got them both on a series of regular injections to ensure the synchronization of their cycles. Everything seemed to happen really fast all of a sudden, after years of thinking about pursuing surrogacy and then months of planning and organizing. Eight eggs were harvested from the egg donor, and we were called in to provide the semen sample. A few days later, we had a number of healthy embryos ready to be implanted into the surrogate. With the arrival of the big day, we were both nervous and excited. We were also very keen to ensure that we had twins—after all it entailed going through the surrogacy route, having twins seemed to be ideal for us.

We were present at the insertion and urged the doctor to implant three embryos in order to increase the chance of twins. The doctor, however, was of the opinion that the blobs of eight cells we could see on the screen were of excellent quality, and the decision was made to only implant two embryos. There would, in his opinion, be a thirty percent chance of twins. We were hoping for a positive pregnancy with the dream of both embryos implanting.

Seven days later, our surrogate called to say she had done a home pregnancy test which had a positive result. A few days after that, she went into the clinic and a blood test confirmed the pregnancy. At six weeks, we went with the surrogate for the first scan. It was an exciting time, and our excitement doubled when the doctor confirmed that we were expecting twins. We were fortunate that the pregnancy had taken on the first try.

The pregnancy was a roller-coaster ride. We were hoping for the pregnancy to be viable, that both twins would be okay, and that they would reach a decent term. Week after week passed with regular scans and regular contact with the surrogate. Two incidents required hospitalization of the surrogate for a short time but, all things considered, the pregnancy went fairly smoothly. Our babies grew well, and we knew that we were expecting two girls. During this time, we started to prepare a room for the girls and attended a multiple-births parenting seminar which was informative and nerve-racking.

We reached thirty-eight weeks (considered term for twins) and had a C-section date booked. The night before the delivery, we visited our surrogate in the hospital. She was excited and nervous—a feeling that mirrored ours. Early next morning, we arrived at the hospital, changed into scrubs, and went in to [watch the delivery].

The delivery was quick, and we were handed one baby and then the next. At 2.1 kg and 1.9 kg, they were small babies, but perfect and healthy. The relief was immense. We accompanied them down to the maternity ward, where we were both booked in for the duration of the babies' stay in the hospital. Our daughters thrived under the care of the wonderful nurses, and after five days and a plethora of visitors, we headed home with Erin and Ariella. Having twins has been a wonderful and very challenging experience. Both of our girls are doing very well and growing up fast. They are now six years old, and in grade one at their school.

We have carefully considered how we tell our family story, both to them and the world at large—we talk about our family having two parents, like many others, and our gay relationship has meant that we allocate parental roles based on our ability, which has been very liberating. While of course many people are curious or unfamiliar with a gay family like ours, we have generally found, for the most part, a lot of warmth and support, and our children are certainly very well integrated into their school and community. There are fortunately more and more children's books that break the heteronormative and gender-normative stereotypes, and this has been extremely helpful both to our children and to the children that they go to school with.

We first embarked on having children through surrogacy so many years ago, and today it feels like we are just another regular family, with the day-to-day challenges that most families face. What we do know is that being gay doesn't mean not having a family of your own.

CHAPTER 11

HATS

When you first come out or go public with a new identity—be it LGBTQ+ or a massive *Project Runway* fan—there's a novelty and, perhaps once the initial nerves are over, a desire to shout it from the rooftops. And you should, because, eventually, you'll be **proud** of who you are.

I'm already proud of you.

There are days when I think, "God, life would be so much easier if I were straight," but those days are few and far between. I love being gay. I love my freedom. I love making my own rules. I love that I don't have to keep secrets from my friends and family. I love being part of a subculture and a minority group. I even look back on the difficult years at school and feel sorry for how small-minded some of my bullies were. I look at them now and laugh at how sad and TINY their lives are as a result of that.

However, an almost cautionary note to end on:

YOUR IDENTITY IS NOT A DEFINITION.

You are joining this amazing global club filled with awesome people, but you are also just you, and you are **so much more** than just a lesbian, gay, bisexual, queer, or trans person.

OK, you need to imagine yourself as something with lots of parts, perhaps a HARP or a SQUID. You can totally think of your own example. You're basically a HARP SQUID, and one of your tentacles or strings is being lesbian or gay, etc., but you have many more parts.

DO MY HARP SQUID QUIZ. YOU WILL NEED A PENCIL.

- What is your sexual or gender identity?
- What is/was your strongest subject at school?
- What do you cook when you want to impress someone?
- Write a favorite quote from a book or film.
- Tell me one thing only your mother would know about you.
- What's your secret talent?
- Who would play you in the movie of your life?
- If you could do any job in the world, what would it be?
- Who's your best friend (real or imaginary)?
- Where do you see yourself in five years?

You are a complex, multifaceted person. Yes, you. Even if you spend as much time as I do watching *Next Top Model* while eating chocolates, that is still part of what makes you YOU, and it has nothing to do with your sexual identity.

Some of your tentacles will affect your life more than others and, frankly, some are a little weightier than others.

As well as being e.g. gay, you may also be Asian, physically disabled, and a tap dancer. In this instance, the tap-dancing, although fancy, might not define you as much as the other three. This is called **intersectionality**—the study of how much these overlapping identities will influence your life.

However, the fact of the matter is, simply identifying as gay, lesbian, bi, queer, or trans isn't going to get you particularly far by itself. Engaging with a gay scene is fun, but it's not a way of life or, for that many people, a career. If we're honest, it's probably not enormously healthy to spend every waking hour thinking about where your next orgasm is coming from either.

What I'm saying is, now that we've sorted your identity, you're going to have to develop a life. A whole life, of which being LGBTQ+ is just a little bit. Open today's newspaper to the job ads. I'm willing to bet there isn't a full-page splash advertising, **WANTED: GAY PERSON TO BE GAY. FORTY HOURS A WEEK WITH OVERTIME/BENEFITS**.

I'm afraid that, alongside being LGBTQ+, you're in the real world with everyone else. So now that we've used this book to deal with your identity, we need to turn our attention to far bigger issues. Your future, your career, your family, your kids, your aspirations and ambitions. Your hopes and dreams.

Of course, your love life is a deservedly big slice of your

life pie, but if you shunt the homo bit to one side, you're in the same dating pool as everyone else. We're all having the same heartaches, first loves, dumpings, WHY HAVEN'T THEY RETURNED MY TEXT moments, bad dates, and great kisses.

This is the final message. We are NOT in a bitter war with "THE STRAIGHTS." It isn't like that at all. Yeah, there are some homophobic straight people out there, but there are also some deeply homophobic gay people too. Don't go out into the real world thinking all straight people hate you, because they really don't, and you'll only end up limiting yourself to what are essentially LGBTQ+ ghettos.

As LGBTQ+ people gain better rights and higher media visibility, the divide between gay and straight narrows. A generation of small-minded people are basically dying and being replaced by teenagers who grew up on Ellen, Neil Patrick Harris, Michelle Rodriguez, Chris Colfer, and others. Certainly in the West, although we have a long way to go, things are better for LGBTQ+ people than they ever have been.

That said, I don't want you to be too comfortable. The hardest chapter in this book to write was the one about the political situations around the world—most countries are changing for the better, but some regimes are changing for the worse. YOU will have to fight that because, love him,

Dan Savage won't be around forever. Yeah, YOU. YOU need to help. Back of this book: Amnesty, Kaleidoscope, GLAAD, The Trevor Project. Help 'em out. With each generation, things are getting better for LGBTQ+ people—what will YOU do to make sure this continues to happen?

I like to think that, before long, you'll introduce yourself as "a dancer," "a fan," "a friend," "a writer," or "a personal trainer" before, "I'm Bob and I'm gay." Straight people never have to do this, and neither should we.

Be proud. You have lots of different hats. Wear them all with pride. This is such an exciting time to be LGBTQ+; things are constantly changing and evolving and I, for one, can't wait to see what happens next.

A GUIDE TO RECOGNIZING YOUR GAY SAINTS

As an individual, you will have a wide and varied taste in all things musical, artistic, political, and dramatic. However, there are a number of people (as well as films and TV programs) who transcend normal celebrity to become something far more special—they become GAY ICONS— and that includes icons for gay women and trans people too.

As these icons are not necessarily LGBTQ+ themselves, it's hard to say what makes LGBTQ+ people take each one to our hearts. Is it the aesthetic? Is it the glamour? Is it the personal tragedy or overcoming the odds? Is it the kind hearts or open-mindedness to our cause?

Of course, part of the fun is making your own icons. Sometimes we look to our moms and dads for inspiration, and sometimes it's a best friend. You can't help but be inspired—who inspires you?

That said, there are a few inspirations we nearly all agree on, and they have become associated or embedded in gay culture, so you should really get up to speed, if only to form an opinion either way.

Ladies and gents, here's a brief dictionary of gay icons.

A

ABBA: Swedish pop marriage made in Eurovision, itself a mothership of camp.

Ahnoni: Recording artist and the first transgender woman to be nominated for a Brit Award.

Olly Alexander: Activist, actor and lead singer of Year & Years.

Buck Angel: FTM multitattooed porn star, filmmaker, and activist.

B

Beautiful Thing: 1996 movie written by playwright and screenwriter **Jonathan Harvey.** The film features an incredibly sweet love story between two young men on a London council estate.

Munroe Bergdorf: Transgender model and activist.

Bert and Ernie: The *Sesame Street* couple finally came out on the cover of the *New Yorker* when a key part of the United States' Defense of Marriage Act was struck down by that country's Supreme Court in 2013.

Beyoncé: Look, if you are known worldwide by your first name alone, you automatically qualify.

Chaz Bono: Not only did he come out of Cher's vagina, but he is probably the most high-profile trans male on the planet.

David Bowie: The most high-profile bisexual on the list and probably responsible for bringing genderqueer and androgyny firmly into the limelight. A true icon.

Brokeback Mountain: Heartbreaking Oscar winner about gay shepherds.

C

Cher—Oh, God, she's just CHER. CHER.

Chris Colfer & Darren Criss: Their portrayal of cute *Glee* high schoolers brought gay to mainstream American youth.

Tim Cook: As CEO of Apple, Cook is among the most influential and powerful gay men in the world.

Joan Crawford: If her turn in *Whatever Happened to Baby Jane* doesn't do it for you, her depiction in *Mommy Dearest* will. TINA! BRING ME THE AX.

Quentin Crisp: Writer and raconteur who rose to fame with his book *The Naked Civil Servant*. The godfather of fabulous.

D

Tom Daley: The Olympian announced he was in a relationship with *Milk* scriptwriter Dustin Lance Black in 2013. Fantastically, Daley refused to label his sexuality. How modern.

Bette Davis: The other half of the *Baby Jane* double act and referenced in Madonna's "Vogue" rap.

James Dean: The troubled actor is regarded as having formed the quintessential lesbian "look."

Ellen DeGeneres: Easily the most famous lesbian in the world, Ellen came out on live TV and is now in a high-profile marriage to actress **Portia de Rossi.**

Cara Delevingne: Supermodel, formerly dated actor **Michelle Rodriguez** and singer **St Vincent.**

Marlene Dietrich: Bisexual goddess of the silver screen, known for her killer line in male drag.

Nyle Di Marco: The deaf model and activist won both *America's Next Top Model* and *Dancing with the Stars.*

Beth Ditto: Openly gay, outspoken singer of Gossip and fashion icon.

Divine: Riotous drag queen, died way too young. Star of outrageous films like *Pink Flamingos, Hairspray,* and *Female Trouble.*

Doctor Who: Gay men love the concept of a guy who never gets old, never settles down, and is always accompanied by glamorous young women. Can't think why. Also features Captain Jack Harkness, a bi icon in his own right.

E

Luke Evans: Hollywood actor known for *Beauty and the Beast* and *Girl on the Train*.

F

Jodie Foster: A lesbian icon long before she came out officially in a very odd awards speech in 2013.

Stephen Fry: Much loved for his activism, wit, and honesty about mental health.

G

Judy Garland: Considered by many to be the ultimate gay icon, Garland ticks all the boxes: beauty, the voice, the camp credentials (*The Wizard of Oz*), and a tragic downfall.

H

Kathleen Hanna: Leader of the Riot Grrrl movement and member of queer-friendly bands Bikini Kill and Le Tigre.

Hannah Hart: Influential food YouTuber.

I

Dana International: Another Eurovision alum, Dana was (and arguably is) the most famous trans woman in the media.

J

Lauren Jauregui: The Fifth Harmony singer came out as bi in 2016.

Jazz Jennings: The YouTuber is one of the youngest transgender activists in the world.

Elton John: The flamboyant singer and pianist is now known more for his activism and dedication to his HIV/AIDS foundation.

Grace Jones: Camp, eccentric, high fashion. A living art installation and foreshadower of Gaga.

Owen Jones: Influential political journalist and author.

K

Billie Jean King: The first professional sportswoman to come out as openly gay, in 1981.

Hayley Kiyoko: Singer/songwriter, known to her fans as "Lesbian Jesus."

L

The L Word: Groundbreaking and explicit drama about a group of gay women living in Los Angeles.

Lady Gaga: Although doing nothing David Bowie, Grace Jones, and Madonna hadn't done decades earlier in terms of music and style, Lady Gaga was the first major (and also bi) pop star to throw herself into gay activism.

k d lang: Gay singer and lesbian icon.

Paris Lees: Leading trans journalist, author, and presenter.

Annie Lennox: As well as her past as a gender-bending pop androgyne, Lennox is also a staunch supporter of HIV/ AIDS charities.

David Levithan: American author of *Boy Meets Boy* and *Two Boys Kissing*.

M

Madonna: Madonna has become something of a symbol of female strength: Doing what she wants, saying what she wants, wearing what she wants. Gay men seem to like this a lot.

Ricky Martin: The Latin pop sensation is the new poster gay for same-sex parenthood.

Armistead Maupin: Author of the bestselling and much-loved *Tales of the City* saga, chronicling a diverse group of people in San Francisco.

Ian McKellen: Hollywood's most dignified gay actor, reaching millions in his roles as Gandalf and Magneto. McKellen is also a keen activist for gay rights.

Mean Girls: Dialogue from this film makes up 87 percent of any conversation between gay men.

Bette Midler: Gay-friendly diva who started her career playing in a gay sauna.

Harvey Milk: Openly gay city supervisor of San Francisco who fought for equality and the protection of gay people in their jobs. Assassinated in his prime. A true hero.

Liza Minnelli: Not only does she possess Judy Garland's genes, but she earns her spot through her tumultuous private life and Oscar-winning role in *Cabaret*.

The Minogue sisters: Everyone loves a bit of sibling rivalry. Do you like the perky blond one or the sultry brunette? FIGHT. Kylie was taken to the gays' hearts because of her transformation from bubble-permed soap mechanic to hot-panted pop phenomenon.

Janet Mock: Bestselling transgender author and activist.

N

Martina Navratilova: Openly gay sportsperson and the most successful tennis player of all time.

Hari Nef: Transgender supermodel, actor, and style icon.

O

Rosie O'Donnell: Outspoken lesbian television personality.

Tyler Oakley: Wildly successful YouTube personality.

Frank Ocean: The soul singer came out in 2012, a huge step for a young black guy with connections to the stereotypically homophobic world of hip-hop.

Hanne Gaby Odiele: Supermodel who revealed she is intersex in 2017.

Orange is the New Black: A Netflix Original series that includes representation of gay, bi, and trans characters.

P

Paris Is Burning: 1990 documentary about the ballroom drag scene in NYC, giving the community a whole new vocabulary. "Category IS cultural realness!"

Dorothy Parker: American writer and satirist known for her cutting wit and killer put-downs—an inspiration to all.

Dolly Parton: A countrified version of Cher. A survivor who rose out of nothing to become a one-woman empire.

Sarah Paulson: The *American Horror Story* star is in a relationship with *Legally Blonde* actor **Holland Taylor.**

Kim Petras: Transgender German pop starlet.

Pierre et Gilles: French artists and gay couple known for their flamboyant, hyperreal photo paintings.

Q

Queer as Folk: UK or U.S. TV show depending on which version you're watching. The UK version was enormously groundbreaking at the time with its depiction of gay sex and relationships and made a star of its creator Russell T Davies, who went on to revive *Doctor Who*.

R

Michelle Rodriguez: Was dating supermodel Cara Delevingne. The *Fast and Furious* actor refuses to define her sexual fluidity, saying, "Men are intriguing. So are chicks."

Rebecca Root: The first trans actor to appear as a trans character in BBC sitcom *Boy Meets Girl*.

Ruby Rose: *Orange is the New Black* actor and style icon.

Willow Rosenberg: As played by Alyson Hannigan in *Buffy the Vampire Slayer*, she's one of the best depictions of a young gay woman on prime-time TV.

RuPaul: World-famous drag queen and singer, RuPaul reached a new generation as a mentor on the high camp *RuPaul's Drag Race*. YOU BETTER WERK.

S

Saint Sebastian: Often considered the very first gay icon. Always depicted topless, tormented, and very hot. A muse to many a gay artist.

JD Samson: Moustachioed lesbian icon from Le Tigre.

Sex and the City: Created and written mostly by gay men, this series depicting the lives of four NYC women is now a camp classic. Samantha is bi, Miranda (**Cynthia Nixon**) is gay in real life, and Geri Halliwell pops up in one episode.

Leo Sheng: The trans actor stars in the revived *L-Word: Generation Q*.

Showgirls: Nothing is camper than this "shocking" film about a stripper becoming a Las Vegas showgirl. Learn the script or you'll have little to talk about with gay men. IT'S A VERSAYSE.

Troye Sivan: Singer, actor and YouTube personality.

Dusty Springfield: Soulful, tragic singer. The Amy Winehouse of her era. Also identified as bisexual and unofficially married a woman.

Amandla Stenberg: *The Hunger Games* actor identifies as pansexual and gender nonbinary.

Kristen Stewart: Leading Hollywood actor, star of the *Twilight* franchise, has dated both guys and girls.

Barbra Streisand: Singer and actor. I'm not sure why gay men like her so much, but they really do. Especially American gays.

"Larry Stylinson": Look it up on Tumblr.

Tilda Swinton: Androgynous, mysterious, and flawless actress. A muse to Bowie. Like Cher, she now gets away with "Tilda."

T

George Takei: The *Star Trek* icon is now a leading LGBTQ+ rights activist.

Peter Tatchell: This man has dedicated his life to gay activism. You might not know it, but we all owe this man a drink.

Gareth Thomas: Retired professional rugby player and out gay man. Every out sportsman is driving a wedge into a sealed homophobic door of silence in sport.

Alan Turing: Genius mathematician and code breaker who won us the Second World War. Killed himself following chemical castration. A legend.

W

Lena Waithe: Writer, producer, and actor who became a hero, especially to queer Black youth after winning a 2017 Emmy for *Master of None*.

John Waters: Writer and director of camp classics such as *Hairspray*, *Serial Mom*, and *Pink Flamingos*. Collaborator with Divine.

Sarah Waters: Author known for her use of lesbian characters in the novels *Tipping the Velvet* and *Fingersmith*.

Oscar Wilde: Mega-fabulous Irish author and playwright known for *The Importance of Being Earnest* and *The Picture of Dorian Gray*. Got himself jailed simply for being gay.

Jacqueline Wilson: Award-winning author and former National Ambassador for Young People's Literature.

Oprah Winfrey: Outspoken **NOT LESBIAN** television personality.

Jeanette Winterson: Lesbian author of *Oranges Are Not the Only Fruit*.

Will & Grace: It's not the funniest or most subversive American comedy ever made, but a prime-time sitcom about two gay men in the 1990s and early 2000s was a step in the right direction. Also KAREN WALKER.

Y

Jaboukie Young-White: Born into a Jamaican family, the comedian and writer is a regular on *The Daily Show*.

As time moves on, some of these names will fade and new, exciting voices and minds will fill the list. Straight people don't get asked about "straight icons," and it's not necessarily fair to expect famous LGBTQ+ people to serve as role models for the rest of us—but I think those who DO are helping the world see us a little better.

BLACKLIST AND BOYCOTT

As well as supporting gay-friendly people and organizations, it's also important to blacklist and boycott people and companies who are homophobic or transphobic.

- DO NOT download music from rappers who use the word "faggot." You're paying them to be homophobic.
- DO NOT see films based on books by notable homophobe authors (and don't buy their books).
- DO NOT pay to see comedians who are either outwardly homophobic or add to homophobic myths about the gay community.
- DO NOT travel to countries with poor human rights records.
- DO NOT buy produce from countries with poor human rights records. For example, at the time of writing many LGBTQ+ people are refusing to buy Russian vodka because of that country's discriminatory stance against gays.

I'm not going to list homophobic singers, actors, and personalities here because I'm not giving them the oxygen of publicity. What's reassuring is that once a homophobe has revealed their true colors, they tend to disappear from view.

It's a valuable lesson: No one wants to be associated with a bigot, least of all a record label or a film studio.

BUILD A BRIDGE

Guidance for Parents and Carers of LGBTQ+ Youth

Hey there, parents and caregivers—how's it going? Now, I guess there's a possibility you purchased this book because your progeny identifies as lesbian, bi, gay, queer, curious, or transgender. Perhaps you bought it because you suspect your child may be leaning that way. Either way, I'm glad you did. You have come to the right place.

Being a parent of an LGBTQ+ (that little star represents the full spectrum of sexualities and identities) child is challenging, but only in the way that being a parent is challenging. In the NICEST POSSIBLE WAY, this isn't about you. If you are really worried about WHAT THE NEIGHBORS WILL SAY, then there's not really a lot I can say or do to help you with that, other than tell you to get over it. The days of keeping LGBTQ+ people hidden in closets or bricked up in walls are over.

OK, let's break it down a bit.

Gay or bi son? Is it the sex stuff that's worrying you? Here's the thing—**straight people do butt sex too.** And two girls are pretty much doing what your daughter would be doing with a dude, I'm afraid. Basically NO parent needs a visual of that, so as a race, we all have to buy into the shared delusion that our kids will only ever hold hands until the stork arrives, or else we'll go mental.

Is HIV/AIDS worrying you? It should, but you should worry about your straight kids too—HIV isn't at all picky.

If you teach your kids about ALWAYS using condoms, however, you've done your job.

Do you have a gay or bi daughter? What difference does it make whether she likes girls or guys? Is it the grandkid thing? LOADS of gay people have kids now; you might still get them, you might not!

Or is your child transgender or gender nonbinary? Here, you have a choice: you either let your child express their gender in a way that feels authentic and correct for them, or you insist they go through life feeling hugely uncomfortable. Young people today are perhaps more aware of gender variance than we were when we were young. It figures that more and more young people now question their gender and sexual identity.

The BEST parent in the world would be one who prepared for having a gay child from conception, so that when baby comes into the world, you aren't incorrectly tagging them as straight and cisgender (the gender they are assigned at birth). Be READY for all eventualities.

In the very beginning of this book, I describe overhearing a mother telling her infant that when he's older he'll "kiss girls." Well there's a five percent chance he'll want to kiss boys, so that mother was potentially setting him up for a very difficult adolescence. All a parent needs to do is be HONEST and explain at an early age, in a totally appropriate way, that five percent of people will want to kiss people the same sex as them. I assure you letting children in on this secret is NOT going to "turn them gay." It really, REALLY doesn't work like that. You could do a LOT worse than buying a copy of the gorgeous picture book *And Tango Makes Three* and sharing it with your child.

If you are a parent who is starting to suspect your child may be LBGT*, you would do a fantastic job to let them know how cool you are with that. Let them know, subtly, that you're open-minded; let them know that you're there to listen; don't turn off the TV when lesbians come on. Yeah, that actually happens a lot. Instead, use gay characters on TV as a talking point to display your coolness with the gay community—that way your son or daughter is much more likely to open up to you.

If your child has already come out with their identity, then reading this book will help. It will give you a glimpse into the future—the case studies in this book have been through it all before, and we all survived. What's more, most of us survived with our parental relationships intact, even if there were difficult periods. Unnecessarily difficult, I would argue.

But don't just take it from me. I asked each of the participants in my study what advice they wish they'd given their parents before they came out. Here's what they said:

Educate yourself from reputable sources. Be cool about it, even if you're slightly freaking out inside. And ASK YOUR CHILD what they would like you to say to others, how they would like to be represented to the larger world by you. And then STICK TO THAT. It builds trust with your child and enables them to be comfortable in their life and progress at their own pace. Allow them to control their own narrative.

—Anon, 24, Boston, Massachusetts

Don't force the issue, but take any opportunity to show that you are open to any choice that they want to make. My coming out was about as easy as it gets really, made that way by a mother who never pushed to find out but gave me an opportunity to tell her. Before you come out, it seems like the hardest thing you will ever have to do, and coming to terms with your own sexuality can take time.

—Chris, Manchester, UK

Let them be. That may sound weird, but if they want to talk to you about it, they will. The best thing you can do is try to let them know that you're okay with it (in a subtle way, not saying outright to them, "It's okay if you're gay, you know"). If you're not okay with it, then it's time for you to think about that. Why aren't you okay with it? What's the real problem here?

—Kayla, 21, Winnipeg, Canada

They are still your child, just reimagined. Forcing them back in the closet because you are uncomfortable is a s**tty thing to do. Pretending they are still straight is a crappy thing to do. Making them go to a pray-away-the-gay camp is not only very s**tty but a mentally and emotionally scarring experience. The world does not owe you a straight child; you produced, not reproduced. Is your tantrum over not "getting your way" worth the relationship with your child? You are still allowed to have opinions of your child's partners, like whether they are good people, have goals, make your child happy. You know, like you would if your child were straight.

—Elizabeth, 23, Chicago, Illinois

Wait for them to tell you. If you ask them, they'll freak out. It's not fair to force them to come out to you. If you really want them to trust you, make sure that you create a space in which they feel safe and comfortable talking to you. It is your responsibility to make them feel like they can trust you.

—E, 16, Michigan

> It's a bumpy ride for any child growing up who isn't
> heterosexual, so just listen to them. Allow them to talk
> freely and openly about who they are and respond with
> nothing but love and compassion, and stress to them that
> there is nothing wrong with them.
>
> —Stuart, 33, UK

The survey respondents MAINLY swing to the do NOT try to force it out of your child camp, although a few clearly say they would prefer a more direct route:

> Sometimes asking outright is better than constantly
> hedging around the question. If my mom were to ask me,
> "Are you gay?" or, "Are you bi?" I'd answer honestly. Since
> she's never done that, it's always been a sort of elephant
> in the room for us.
>
> —Stephanie, 24, Pittsburgh, Pennsylvania

I think it's up to you as a parent to know if your child will respond well to a very direct approach.

As a final point, be aware that your child's identity isn't your "fault" and, even if it were, it's no bad thing. I've been trans for a really long time now, and it's pretty good fun. To be honest, in my careers as a teacher and author, it's had very little impact. I used to be in a band, and I did clinical neuropsychology at university. I got a first-class honors degree. My sexuality hasn't held me back EVER.

Your child's identity is a part of them that has always been there. They haven't even changed; it's just that now you're seeing the whole picture—IT'S BUTTERFLY TIME.

THE CHEAT SHEET

All the weird terms, no waiting.

69: Two people giving simultaneous oral sex.

AIDS: A syndrome brought on by the virus HIV.

Aromantic: A person who experiences little to no romantic attraction.

Asexual: A person who is not interested in sex or has low sexual desire.

Bisexual: A person who fancies both men and women.

Blow job: Oral sex on a guy.

Bottom/passive: Being the partner who "receives" during sex.

Circumcised: Term to describe a boy who has had his foreskin surgically removed.

Cisgender: The sex you were assigned at birth.

Clitoris: Female erogenous zone.

Coming out: The process of telling people about your identity.

Cum: Common slang term for semen OR to orgasm.

Cunnilingus: Oral sex on a girl.

Curious/questioning: A person in the process of wondering about their sexuality.

Dildo: A sex toy.

Dom: Being the dominant partner during sex.

Douching: Washing out the back passage or lady garden prior to sex.

Drag queen/king: A performer who wears clothes traditionally assigned to the opposite gender.

Fellatio: Fancy term for oral sex on a dude.

Foreskin: Loose skin at the end of the penis.

Gay: Term to describe a homosexual man or woman.

Genderqueer: A person who identifies with neither, both, or a combination of male and female genders.

Glory hole: A hole in a wall or partition through which a man pokes his peenie.

Grindr: A social network app for gay and bi men.

HIV: A virus affecting the immune system.

Intersectionality: The different parts of your whole identity and the impact they have on your life.

Intersex: Term to describe a person born with no clear gender or attributes of both genders.

Labia: The folds at the entrance of the vagina.

Lesbian: A homosexual woman.

Lube: Short for lubricant. Makes sex easier.

Orgasm: Sexual climax.

Orgy: Group sex.

Penis: Male erogenous zone.

Poppers: Slang term for amyl nitrite—an aroma that gives a feeling of light-headedness.

Queer/genderqueer: A person who refuses to label their sexuality or gender.

Rimming: Licking the bottom.

Scat: Eating poop.

Scissor sisters: A sexual position for two women OR an early 2000s electropop band.

Strap-on: A sex toy worn on a belt.

STI: Sexually transmitted infection.

Sub: Being the submissive partner during sex.

Top/active: Being the partner who "gives" during sex.

Transsexual: Any person changing their gender identity.

Transvestite: A person who wears the clothes traditionally assigned to the opposite gender.

Vibrator: A vibrating sex toy.

Water sports/golden shower: Peeing on people in a way considered sexy.

Helpful Numbers and Websites and Stuff

You are not alone. The Internet is jam-packed with services especially for young LGBTQ+ people. The aim is to provide you with information, friends, contacts, and condoms. Obviously, Google is your best friend, but here are some links and numbers to save you some time.

HELPLINES

The Trevor Lifeline, part of the Trevor Project: Offers crisis intervention, suicide prevention, and community resources, among their services.

1-866-488-7386

thetrevorproject.org

The GLBT National Help Center offers peer counseling and local resources, among their services.

For youth, 25 and under: **1-800-246-PRIDE (1-800-246-7743)**

For all ages: **1-888-843-4564**

glbtnationalhelpcenter.org

CHARITIES AND PRESSURE GROUPS

Gay & Lesbian Alliance Against Defamation (GLAAD): glaad.org

Gay, Lesbian & Straight Education Network (GLSEN): glsen.org

Gay-Straight Alliance Network (GSA): gsanetwork.org

The Kaleidoscope Trust: kaleidoscopetrust.com

Amnesty International: amnestyusa.org

Human Rights Campaign: hrc.org

Trans Youth Equality Foundation: transyouthequality.org

LGBTQ+ YOUTH GROUPS

National Youth Advocacy Coalition: nyacyouth.org

Youth Resource: youthresource.org

DISCRIMINATION AND BULLYING

It Gets Better Project: itgetsbetter.org

StopBullying.gov: stopbullying.gov/at-risk/groups/lgbt/index.html

Lambda Legal: lambdalegal.org

SEXUAL HEALTH

Center for Disease Control and Prevention: cdc.gov/sexualhealth/ and cdc.gov/lgbthealth/

Aids.gov; aids.org

National LGBT and Health Education Center: lgbthealtheducation.org

MARRIAGE ADVOCACY GROUPS

Freedom to Marry: freedomtomarry.org

Marriage Equality USA: marriageequality.org

This is by no means a complete list. New groups are starting all the time, and it's likely there's a youth group very close to where you live.

Acknowledgments

So many people to thank on this one. Firstly a big thank you to everyone who contributed both their time and their stories to this book. I simply wouldn't have done it without you, seriously. Special thanks to All Sorts Youth Group in Brighton and Wayne Dhesi at Stonewall.

Thanks again to Tori Kosara, my UK editor, who suggested the project in the first place and also supported it throughout. I wasn't sure there was a book here, but it turns out there is, and it's one I think we can both be proud of. The fantastic illustrations are once again down to Spike Gerrell and I think you've brought the words to life.

Thanks to everyone at Hot Key and Red Lemon. Nonfiction is such a team effort. Thanks to Jet and Dan for the cover and design and to Emma for overseeing everything. SPAM team: love you long time.

Huge thanks to David Levithan for his beautiful foreword, and to Annette Pollert-Morgan and everyone at Sourcebooks Fire for understanding what I wanted to achieve with *This Book Is Gay* and sharing it with the States!

When I was writing *This Book Is Gay* I could only HOPE that the message would reach so far.

Finally, thanks as ever to Jo, my fantastic agent!

About the Author

Juno Dawson is a bestselling novelist, screenwriter, journalist, and columnist for *Attitude* magazine. Her writing has appeared in *Glamour*, *The Pool*, *Dazed*, and the *Guardian*. She has appeared on *Pointless Celebrities*, BBC Women's Hour, *Front Row*, ITV News, Channel 5 News, *This Morning*, and *Newsnight*. Juno's books include the global bestsellers *This Book Is Gay* and *Clean*. She won the 2020 YA Book Prize for *Meat Market*. She also writes for television and has multiple shows in development both in the UK and the U.S. An occasional actress and model, Juno had a cameo in the BBC's *I May Destroy You* (2020) and was the face of Jecca Cosmetics Play Pots campaign.

Juno grew up in West Yorkshire, writing imaginary

episodes of *Doctor Who*. She later turned her talent to journalism, interviewing luminaries such as Steps and Atomic Kitten, before writing a weekly serial in a Brighton newspaper.

Juno lives in Brighton. She is a part of the queer cabaret collective known as Club Silencio. In 2014, Juno became a School Role Model for the charity Stonewall.